Monsters Under the Bed

Monsters Und is an essential text focusing on critical and contemporary issues surrounding v t r early years children. Containing a critically creative and a creatively critica i n ion of the cult and culture of the child and childhood in fiction and non-fic ion writing, it also contains a wealth of ideas and critical advice.

This text dynamic ly explores the issues of picture books, literacy and writing for early years children with wider view on child-centred culture, communication and media. Internationally reco nised as an expert in the field, Andrew Melrose encourages academics, researchers and students to examine the fundamental questions in writing for and addressing early year ch n, through an exploration of text and images. Accessibly written and lively in its a ach, the book includes:

- critically impor lenge to the latest international academic research and debates in the idren's literature and creative writing;
- an extensive i of early years writing and reading;
- a pathway t critical awareness of children's literature, allowing students to develop ical ability and writing skills;
- constant 'c' roughout, in which the reader is encouraged to reflect on creatively ment.

Providing pedagogical approach, this compelling text will be an indispensa ics, writers and students interested in writing for children, as well a riting, children's literature and English BA and MA programme it interest to those in teacher training, PGCE students and those ost-Doctoral level.

Andrew Writing for Children at the University of Winchester. He has a *Children* and *Here Comes the Bogeyman*, published by Routledge.

Monsters Under the Bed

Critically investigating early years writing

Andrew Melrose

Routledge
Taylor & Francis Group

LONDON AND NEW YORK

First published 2012
by Routledge
2 Park Square, Milton Park, Abingdon, Oxon OX14 4RN

Simultaneously published in the USA and Canada
by Routledge
711 Third Avenue, New York, NY 10017

Routledge is an imprint of the Taylor & Francis Group, an informa business

British Library Cataloguing in Publication Data
A catalogue record for this book is available from the British Library

Library of Congress Cataloging-in-Publication Data
Melrose, Andrew, 1954–
Monsters under the bed: critically investigating early years writing / Andrew Melrose.
    p. cm.
    Includes bibliographical references.
1. Children's literature–Authorship. 2. Children in literature. I. Title.
PN147.5.M44 2012
808.06'8–dc23   2011035943

ISBN: 978–0–415–61749–9 (hbk)
ISBN: 978–0–415–61750–5 (pbk)
ISBN: 978–0–203–13677–5 (ebk)

Typeset in Bembo
by Swales & Willis Ltd, Exeter, Devon

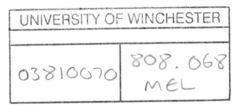

MIX
Paper from
responsible sources
FSC
www.fsc.org   FSC® C004839

Printed and bound in Great Britain by
TJ International Ltd, Padstow, Cornwall

Contents

Acknowledgements

Writing is a solitary job and yet a writer never writes alone; many people helped to make this book possible. Thank you to Alison Foyle who commissioned it and has been especially helpful throughout. Thanks also to the University of Winchester for supporting the research through their Research and Knowledge Exchange fund and to colleagues in the Department of English, Creative Writing and American Studies for their encouragement and support – in particular Mick Jardine, Inga Bryden, Neil McCaw, Judy Waite, Jill Barnes, Leonie Lipton, Ian Roberts and Judith Heneghan who runs the MA Writing for Children. Vanessa Harbour, University of Winchester, and Jen Webb, University of Canberra, allowed me to bounce ideas off them – and they always bounced back better than they left. A great deal of the intellectual energy and thought behind this book developed through my work with Karenanne Knight, who also designed the cover (and the cover of the sister book to this, *Here Comes the Bogeyman*). Many thanks also to Stephanie Morris who illustrated the 'mother and child with book'. My family, Diane, Abbi and Daniel, have been brilliant; they continue to give me space, time and love in their busy lives and it is appropriate that this book is dedicated to them.

Introduction

Artists, writers and critics engaged in ideas on child-centred culture, communication and media tend to throw the terms 'child' and 'children' and 'young people' out as interchangeable expressions that describe those people below the age of eighteen (in the UK certainly) without really thinking. Yet using these terms as if they were synonymous is far from ideal, for the terms themselves are subject to other descriptors as diverse as gender, race, socioeconomic status and many further subdivisions. But what can be said is that the people we call children are temporarily the inexperienced branch of the human family. And in acknowledging this, I will be picking up on the proposal that experience is gained through a process of joint activity, where attending, remembering and reasoning are things done between people. Most powerfully, they are done between experts and novices, teachers and learners (Crook 2008: 32)[1] and, I would contend, the experts and teachers are joined by writers, artists and creators of story narrative: because important for me in the proposal is the idea of 'joint activity' between the experienced and the less so and between the critically creative and creatively critical discourse. Deleuze is right here to say,

> The relationships between theory and practice are far more partial and fragmentary. Practice is a set of relays from one theoretical point to another, and theory is a relay from one practice to another. No theory can develop without eventually encountering a wall, and practice is necessary for piercing this wall.
>
> (Deleuze, in Foucault and Deleuze 1972: 2)

Later on I will call it 'exploring the connections' and we will look at that idea in depth, because the exciting challenge in a book like this is to explore the connections in the joint activity, which is fundamental to the underpinning of authentic, child-centred discourse. Indeed, the term 'child-centred discourse' will also come under scrutiny, as will the cult and culture that is the child and childhood because these concepts are too complex to be treated as simply being interchangeable words.

Throughout this book I propose to unfold some of the *cultural, critical* and *creative* ideas that surround the underpinning issues in child-centred discourse so that once they are contextualised they will not look as strange as they do now. The book is split into two distinct sections:

- **Part I** plots a path through the critical and cultural context surrounding the ongoing 'theoretical' debates on child-centred culture, communication and media; the critical context in summarising the critical discourse and arguments that have ensued over the past thirty years or so; looking at ways of taking the arguments and debates forward and then concluding by aiming to reveal a *new way of seeing* from a critical and creative perspective.

- **Part II** concentrates on the creative aspect in the (im)possibility of child–centred culture, communication and media, with a view to negotiating critically creative and creatively critical strategies involved in the process. In Deleuzian terms it is the discourse of 'practice'.

Part I

Chapter 1

Monsters under the bed

If you mention the idea of writing for 'early years' in most social or academic circles the immediate reaction is usually that you are writing about little books for little people. But the complexities surrounding ideas on child-centred culture, communication and media discourses are much thornier than this simple explanation provides. The cult and culture that is a child and childhood is a highly developed industry and a lot of the critical material targeted at the practice of writing for children (in books, film and television) overlaps with this wider picture on critical and cultural transmission and the complexities of the cultural field of production, which cannot be separated or critiqued in isolation from many of the other component parts (although not everyone agrees with me on this).[1]

But I also use the phrase 'the cult and culture of the child and childhood' in a slightly provocative way in order to try and highlight that the unusualness of the discourse surrounding the relevant issues can often look a little eccentric. For example, phrases such as the 'constructed child' and 'constructive child' surface as explanatory critical issues, and I will come on to this in time.

But going back to little books for little people, what chance does a picture book have to be a force for good in the life of a developing child? It is such a small thing, no more than a fragment of paper in the history of printing, how can it survive the age of electronic imagery, television and the advancing computer and internet technology? Indeed why should it survive: is it not already redundant, already anachronism? After all, as Jack Zipes says, it gets buried under so much other stuff, and no better phrase is necessary here:

> It is simply impossible to discuss children and children's literature today without situating them within the complex of the cultural field of production in which young people are introduced to a variety of commodities connected to a book, story, or poem that they are reading. When a child encounters a book, often mediated by a teacher, librarian, parent, or a friend, the relationship with the book is no longer the young reader and the text, but young consumer and a myriad of products associated with the text that the child will be encouraged to buy and to buy more of the same: video tapes, CDs, DVDs, games, dolls, t-shirts, watches, cups, clothing, food, and so on.
>
> (Zipes 2009: 1)

Indeed what chance the book itself when Zipes had previously written, 'I am not being coy – children's literature does not exist' (Zipes 2002: 40). These are not issues easily dismissed and I will not do so here. But what I will do is defend the book element of culture, communication and media ideas that are early child-centred because I think the book is indeed very important to early years development.

This is especially relevant since recent figures in London show that one in three children in the city do not own a book, one in four leaves primary school unable to read or write properly and one in five leaves the school system altogether unable to read or write with confidence. Should the book survive amidst the advance of electronic media and consumer placement? Of course it should and must. What I will try to do throughout is emphasise why and I will propose a new way of seeing and thinking about this because while picture books are very important to children's early engagement with art, culture, communication and media, they are a very important component in the exploration of their learning life which will forever be influenced by the same art, culture, communication and media, and their literacy amidst the maelstrom is crucial.

In saying children's literature does not exist, Zipes was addressing a complex, critical discourse in media, culture and communication and a huge intellectual deliberation on the cult and culture that is a child and childhood. It would be foolish to ignore it because this notion, and its wider significance, has been prevalent in child and children debates over the past thirty years or so. To many of the critics involved in the surrounding deliberations, it is a statement that hardly holds any controversy whatsoever (although that is not to say there is consensus and agreement: the enquiry is young and ongoing). Furthermore, just because I am entering this debate via picture books, in the first instance, it doesn't just apply to children's literature but to the wider discourse that is adult-made and child-centred, and this idea will be expanded upon later because it is extremely important to the entire critical understanding of early years.

Some of the underlying issues have already been addressed in greater detail in *Here Comes the Bogeyman: Exploring Contemporary Issues in Writing for Children* (Melrose 2011), which is a sister book to this one. But some of the concerns cross over and need to be (re)rehearsed here because there is much to contextualise and understand. The important thing to record is that the critical discourse has much more to do with cultural and communication ideas and ideology rather than literary studies. The cult of the 'child', 'children' and 'childhood', the culture of the 'child', 'children' and 'childhood' and the idea of cultural transmission and communication with children are much more complex than simply producing a picture book or an animation film (say) and sending it out for them to engage with.

It is clear that in this still new twenty-first century children, young people, are being defined more and more by the idea of the 'cult' and 'culture' of childhood being created through adult given, *children-centred* commodification, advertised lifestyles, media and an unalienable cultural crisis wrapped up in the irrepressible rise of capitalism. And much of the work done by Jack Zipes concentrates on revealing and critiquing this. But for a storyteller in cultural practice, to be aware of it allows for a certain amount of resistance, which this book will propose (in time) although we need to look at it the issues in more detail.

In her fascinating and useful critical insight on writing for children and her explanation of what she calls *aetonormativity* (Lat. *aeto* – pertaining to age and *normative* – pertaining to implying, creating, or prescribing a norm or standard), Maria Nikolajeva reminds us that the 'child/adult imbalance is most tangibly manifested in the relationship between the ostensibly adult narrative voice and the child focalizing character' (2010: 8). Which means that, essentially, nowhere else are power structures as obvious as they are in the relationship between adults and children through home, health, education, educators, extended family, social and cultural exchanges, and in the culture adults produce for children, such as books, toys, television shows etc., all of which are created by those in power for the powerless. In this sense, too, the idea of the 'expert' in this relationship does not make life any easier for critics to address because the *only* qualification required to be such an expert is to be an adult.

But this normativity issue is complex and needs to be explored further because the whole concept of the cult and culture of the child is essentially wrapped up in two main ideas which can conveniently be called the 'constructive' and the 'constructed' child. A reading of Michel Foucault is a useful place to begin opening the details of this debate out:

> categories such as 'childhood' were generally understood as being stable ('everybody knows what a child is'), in reality they were subject to transformation and revision as new forms of knowledge were developed . . . the 'truth' of childhood (and doubtless the same applies to categories such as adolescence and youth) can be understood as both stable and unproblematic, on the one hand ('the truth of childhood is the sum of those knowledges that take it as their object') and, more problematically, as a site of discursive and institutional 'battles' (and therefore lacking in final authorization, not the truth but a set of 'truths') . . . while we all think we know what a child or adolescent is, in fact these categories have histories . . . and are always in the process of being transformed.
>
> (Danahaer, Schirato and Webb 2000: 78)

The idea of 'always in the process of being transformed' is simple enough to negotiate. My childhood is markedly different from the one my own children, now fifteen and seventeen, have experienced and are about to leave. But they, too, look to younger cousins and can see the marked difference in the childhood those children are experiencing from their own. And each succeeding generation will be able to look at this in similar ways. The world changes, nothing ever remains static but this does not mean we cannot, to some extent, collate a common set of thoughtful ideas with this in mind.

However, the issues of categories and histories and ongoing transformation are problematised further by a discernible disagreement: 'on the one hand . . .', writes Rudd, 'there is an underlying "essential" child whose nature and needs we can know and, on the other, the notion that the child is nothing but the product of adult discourse (as some social constructionists argue)' (Rudd 2004: 29–30), which is to say there are two definitions of child as 'constructive' or 'constructed' or even a combination of the two. This is highlighted where most modern-day sociologists appear to insist that childhood is socially constructed rather than being fundamental to the state of being; whereas developing psychologists appear to see childhood as defined in large part by the state of being a child and focus attention on the complex process of individual development and I have seen some critics describe them as a hybrid of the two, which I suspect is nearer to being the case. I will not be exploring this at great length, though. The issues are complex and the research vast, but I am persuaded by ideas that suggest the cognitive development in children is experience-dependent. As Goswami (2008: 1–2; cf. Livingstone 2009: 16–17) writes:

It is now recognized that children think and reason in the *same* ways as adults from early childhood. Children are less efficient reasoners than adults because they are more easily misled in their logic by interfering variables such as contextual variables, and because they are worse at inhibiting information . . . The major developmental change during the primary years is the development of self-regulatory skills . . . Cognitive development is experience-dependent, and older children have had more experiences than younger children . . .

As I said above, I will be picking up on the radical proposal that experience is gained through a process of joint activity, where attending, remembering and reasoning are things done between people, and picture books and writing for early years come in right at the beginning of this process as exemplars of both actual and vicarious experience. Children are not passive observers but active participators in cultural experience and this will be explained at length as I progress.

And yet this too is problematised by some other critical ideas on writing for children which begin with Jacqueline Rose's contentious though important reading of *Peter Pan*. There is much to be said about Rose's work – and much has been said already, for she has her supporters and detractors. I am taking it up here because it repeats Zipes' contention, where she states,

Children's fiction is impossible, not in the sense that it cannot be written (that would be nonsense), but in that it hangs on an impossibility, one which rarely speaks. This is the impossible relation between adult and child . . . Children's fiction is clearly about the relation [between adult and child], but it has remarkable characteristics of being about something which it hardly ever talks of. Children's fiction sets up a world in which the adult comes first (author, maker, giver) and the child comes after (reader, product, receiver), *but where neither of them enter the space in between* [my italics].

(Rose 1984: 1–2)

This has also been exposed to critical scrutiny and at great length in *Here Comes the Bogeyman* (Melrose 2011), and there isn't enough space in this book to go into the detail which that other book does. But a summary of the ideas need to be addressed before we proceed because it is crucial to understanding the idea of cultural transmission and communication in the writing for early years.

So let's begin by saying that the entire premise of Rose's assertion can be countered very simply. The 'impossible relation between adult and child' and the idea that neither can enter the 'space in-between' them is both ideologically and sociologically unsound. This is because the gap, the space in-between, is the same as between you and me, simply one of experience. The gap is between the child and the adult's experience, between the experience of adult authority and the child's inexperience and the job of the storyteller and of story is to negotiate the gap; just as the child reaches into the space so too does the writer. Of course, this is not without its problems too and these need also to be addressed.

Maria Nikolajeva reminds us that, 'As adults – writers as well as promoters of children's literature – we cannot unconditionally abolish adult normativity' (Nikolajeva 2010: 204). Yet we can think about how books (say, though it could equally be film, art and so on) negotiate the production of a 'social and aesthetic transformation of culture' for children (Reynolds 2009: 99)[2] and indeed (re)negotiate the constitution of what is normative.

Although this is not straightforward and the experiential gap between the adult and the child has to be understood in context. What Rose does with her idea of adult normativity is identify the child as 'other' which replicates that master/servant; oppressor/oppressed; male/female idea of normative power and its easy to see how adult/child can slip into this binary idea.

But labelling the child as 'other', in the same analogue as women, gay, people of colour etc., is just not a convincing argument for me. Michel Foucault writes, 'For a thing to be different, it must first no longer be the same; and it is on this negative basis, above the shadowy part that delimits the same, that contrary predicates are then articulated' (Foucault 1970: 183–4). The reason children cannot be other is simple; they occupy a radically different social space, and this is because theirs is contingent and genuinely temporary, in a way that is only ever shadowed in all the other demographic categories. They truly are in a process of becoming, not being, the woman, the black person, the gay, etc. Those other demographic categories are pretty much stuck with their markers. But a child is an identity under erasure; the child only has a few years before he or she is camouflaged as 'one of us'. And those marked groups are conspicuous on the basis of their morphology, made up of its interconnected or interdependent parts, while the child is marked more on the basis of their stage of socialisation and their neurological capacity alongside those interconnected or interdependent parts.

Also the members of those groups have (wittingly or otherwise) entered the social contract, while the child has not yet reached that stage. Thus, we have to think about this differently because Rose's reading just feels outdated and wrong. Children's fiction does indeed set up 'a world in which the adult comes first (author, maker, giver) and the child comes after (reader, product, receiver)' but mutual negotiation is taking place. The child is not coming to a text blankly; they are coming as intelligent social beings who are growing more intelligent by the minute.

Critically speaking, Jacques Derrida's ideas around the word *différance* is useful here (1982: 1–27). *Différance* plays on the fact that the French word *différer* doesn't translate into a single English meaning but comes to mean both to 'differ' and 'defer' and in this sense we can see how children can be accommodated in this way. According to Althussar in his posthumously published 'Letters to D.', 'The child irrupts as a biological being within the system of the symbolic order' (see Phillips 2002: 152). Children differ from adults, that is obvious, but they are not other, they are just not yet the same; the difference is only one of experience and their catch-up is deferred only by experience which they will gain in time.

There is a way of trying to explain this but we have to take a detour. Homi Bhabha, who writes on post-colonialism and post-colonial theory, gives us a way in (if not all of the answers) when he addresses this space between the adult and the child referred to by Rose. Bhabha is talking about the coloniser and colonial subject here but the ideas can be explored (and I would ask you to hang on to that word – explored):

> we should remember that it is the 'inter' – the cutting edge of translation and negotiation, the *in between* space – that carries the burden of the meaning of culture . . . by *exploring* [as opposed to dominating] this Third Space, we may elude the politics of polarity [adult/child in our case] and emerge as the others of our selves [italics and intervention mine].

> (Bhabha 1994: 38)

The additional italic and editing serves to help with the explanation but from this small quotation we can suddenly see the whole issue take on a new focus. This is because this 'in-between space', also referred to by Rose, remember, is negotiated by *exploring* as opposed to being rendered *impossible* to enter. And this is hugely different take on Rose's is equally and hugely significant. It does need more exploration and explanation (see *Here Comes the Bogeyman*) but surely *exploring* the radically different experiential but real social space that exists between adult and child, who is contingent and genuinely temporary, where the adult, via a text can visit the 'exploring' child rather than have the child come to the text to be dominated by it and the adult producer is a real and radical prospect. What is actually taking place is that the adult is articulating for children, while and at the same time children who already know more than they can articulate are learning how to articulate their own story, while also learning something new.

Thus, critics of writing for children should be made aware that the responsible job of writing for children, the job of the responsible writer, the artist, the storyteller is to explore the same gap, the in-between space, by providing a story which allows it to be bridged. A child needs to be able to 'explore' the boundaries of its own knowledge in the mediated 'space in-between'. But this child doesn't arrive in ignorance, even at a very young age. The child comes to confirm what it already knows, even if he/she cannot yet articulate it – for all children know more than they can articulate. But the child also comes to get to know more, to find out what he or she knows not. And this too needs further extrapolation here.

Of course, the idea that there is no such thing as children's fiction is true (up to a point – see Reynolds 2007: 180–3). It is true to say children's literature is written for them and not by them. But this is surely a rather pedantic reading of the possessive apostrophe in *children's*. Surely it is possible to re-conceive the apostrophe as rendering not the 'possessive' but the 'associative' – so that it refers not to literature owned by children, but literature connotatively and indeed denotatively part of the domain of children/childhood/the child state.[3] I think it is probably a clearer interpretation of the options on offer, and that in fact in the montage of culture, communication and media convention it is simply an adult created, *child-centred discourse*, the politics of which are in constant (re)negotiation.

What also has to be recognised is that childhood is not the opposite of adulthood; it is not solved by adulthood; it is not preparation for adulthood, it is childhood and children (young people, young persons) are children (young people, young persons) not apprentice adults; children occupy a radically different social space from the adult because theirs is contingent and genuinely temporary as they stride through childhood, teenagehood into young adulthood and the meeting in the in-between space is an ideal site for exploration as they gather experience on the journey. You might ask: how is this meeting negotiated though? Well, knowing about it helps but let's think it through.

Rightly, I feel, the children's psychoanalyst Adam Phillips observes that:

> Children unavoidably treat their parents as though they were experts on life . . . but children make demands on adults which adults don't know what to do with . . . once they [children] learn to talk they create, and suffer, a certain unease about what they can do with words. Paradoxically, it is the adult's own currency – words – that reveals to them the limits of adult authority . . . Adults can nurture children . . . but they do not have the answers . . . *what they can do is tell children stories about the connections . . .*
>
> (Phillips 1995: 1–2)

The in-between space is the site of nurture, where the connections are made through stories. There is a stark simplicity to this and once again it comes up against the idea that, *children understand more than they can articulate at all the stages of their life*, where-minute-by-minute, hour-by-hour, day-by-day they supplement their knowledge and experience with the new. Rebecca Lowe argues: 'I firmly believe that an adult can never hope to understand a child's mind; the differences are just too fundamental . . .' but then she spends most of her fascinating book precisely and deliberately recording the 'connections' (Lowe 2007: 167).

But surely we all do! Surely we all of us come to a book, a text, a film, a website, etc., knowing what we already know, even if the writer of the content, issues, ideas, etc., can articulate it better than we could expect, while and at the same time we are all looking for something new. It is the human condition; it is about making critically creative and creatively critical connections. It is the story of a self-conscious engagement with narrative, experimenting with form and processes that are still being shown to be connected to older stories and art forms, from whence they came as they are taken forward. It is not even a new idea and can be traced back to Socrates, 469–399 BC. It's not so much explaining or showing but helping others to connect to what they already know from other parts of life and then asking them to take the ideas forward into something they may or may not have thought about but are ready to explore. The child will take the story you have offered and incorporate it with their own thinking to take possession of the knowledge the mutual exploration imparts – it is nurture in progress. As Philippa Pearce once said,

> I used to think – and to say in print – that authors of children's books usually wrote out of childhood experience, that I myself certainly did. Now I am not so sure. Almost, I'm sure not. That is, I think I write out of present experience, but present experience includes – sometimes painfully – the past.
>
> (Pearce, in Meek, Warlow and Barton 1977: 182)

And is it not a true Socratic journey? As Jameson might have added, although he was commenting on some Lacanian ideas on reality and language:

> Personal identity is itself the effect of a certain temporal unification of past and future with one's present and . . . such active unification is itself a function of language, or better still of the sentence.
>
> (Jameson 1991: 27)

And likewise, while Webb and Krauth (2010) are not speaking specifically about child-centred discourse their intervention on the relationship between images and words is relevant and enables me to strengthen the ideas I am proposing. This is part of their editorial introduction to an edition of TEXT Journal, which I contributed to:[4]

> It is timely to attend to the embodied nature of writing and of reading, and to the *relationship* evident between images and words. The latter is a topic that emerges in the literature time and again, though it never seems to be fully resolved, while the former slips in and out of currency. On the one hand, new research, especially into cognition, reveals the centrality of our embodied status to how we think, move and

find our being in the world. On the other hand, in the light of what we witness in popular culture, popular science and popular warfare it seems almost that the embodied human is going out of fashion, in favour of the possibilities offered by the digital world that inflect our understandings of what it means to be human . . . we can be both, simultaneously – living, breathing, feeling and fully material subjects; and abstract 'paper' subjects who are constituted, and constitute ourselves, in language.

Socrates never claimed to be wise, only to understand the path a lover of wisdom must take in pursuing it. It is such a simple idea. It can be a path through the forest, a mountain to climb, a sea to swim, a journey through the labyrinth, for are critics and practitioners of culture, media, art and literature not engaged in this very exercise? Pierre Bourdieu sums up the complexities of our multiple being, describing it as

> this body which indisputably functions as the principle of individuation (in as much as it localizes in space and time, separates, isolates, etc.), ratified and reinforced by the legal definition of the individual as an abstract, interchangeable being, without qualities, is also – as a real agent, that is to say, as a habitus, with its history, its incorporated properties – . . . open to the world, and therefore exposed to the world, and so capable of being conditioned by the world, shaped by the material and cultural conditions of existence in which it is placed from the beginning.
> (Bourdieu 2000: 133–4)

The terminology doesn't matter, it can be the archaeological dig for the bones of knowledge that lie buried under piles of words and images which the cultural practitioner has prepared, and it all comes to the same thing; we take the story that is offered and incorporate it with that which we already know while exploring that which we know not, whether we are reading *Can't You Sleep Little Bear* or the margins of philosophy in the works of Slavoj Žižek after Jacques Derrida.

It is in this sense then that the experience of the writer, the artist, the parent may help the child expand his or her field of vision through the vicarious experience that can be negotiated by cultural narrative at the meeting place, in the space in-between. But so too with a child, for does the adult have nothing to gain or to learn from the less experienced? Indeed surely it is modernism acknowledging its historical antecedents in creating the new – the artistic narrative, the story, is surely one about connecting the experience of past times for a new audience. Out of the old comes the new, as Brecht would say. It is not some postmodern end of history or a death of the story narrative and the storyteller but new ways of colluding and adapting to ever-increasing demands of delivery, it is the exploration of life itself taking place in the space in-between. If I am engaged in child-centred art I would be a foolish artist to think I was the only person in the space, would I not? The worst thing anyone can do is to fail to locate the child and to fail to try and understand child understanding. Margaret Meek puts it this way:

> although it is possible to judge books for children by what are called 'adult standards' and regard them as part of literature, the young reader carries a different world in his [her] head, no less complex than an adult's but differently organized. He [she] needs his [her] stories in a different way, his [her] experiences of reading must be different.

When discussing stories for children, to lose sight of the reader is too dangerous to contemplate.

(Meek, Warlow and Barton 1977: 11)

And there is a lot of truth in this idea, as I will go on to explore because it is very important in child-centred discourse.

Walter Benjamin might have referred to this as the trading of experiences, the *Erfahrung*, where the shift between 'lived through' and 'narratable experience' is seen as a point of arbitration and negotiation, an exploration of ideas, the place where the two can meet for mutual benefit. For the writer, Dorothea Brande has a simple take on this which accords well: 'It is well to understand as early as possible in one's writing life that there is just one contribution which every one of us can make: we can give into the common pool of experience some comprehension of the world as it looks to each of us' (Brande 1934: 120).

In this sense, the cultural product of writing for children, such as the picture book, is central to the intimate relationship of nurture and experience in finding out the connections in the stories that make up our lives. Although, at the moment the child engages with the text, the adult writer (storyteller) is getting ready to stand aside, eventually making her or himself absent in the knowledge that the child has not come to the text in ignorance but as a knowing person who is curious to know more about the connections. But this also comes with its own problems. And I say 'getting ready' to stand aside because the intimate connection is not so easy to let go when there are young children involved. The next section will explain this in greater detail.

Chapter 2

Picture books (re)defined

Picture books have to be regarded as one of the great conundrums in an adult-created, *child-centred discourse*. They are not literature but contain great stories with great literary merit; they are not books of art but contain some of the most artistic pictures imaginable; they are in fact an amalgamation, a blending of the two, and yet the words 'picture story books' and 'story picture books' hardly describe them at all. Nikolajeva and Scott (2006: 8) took the step of adopting the word 'picturebook' to distinguish them from 'picture books' or 'books with pictures' and this seems to be a good and logical place to begin with a critical perspective. But in doing so, it is important to point out that the prominent critical debates, bookended by Nodelman (1988) and Nikolajeva and Scott (2006), will be challenged by a single but hitherto important discussion from the writer/artist/critic involved in this critically creative and creatively critical study of the picture book, which will seek to reveal a new way of (re)defining it.

To begin this process, it is important to look at those bookended ideas. Nikolajeva and Scott commented that, 'Nodelman's book provides an excellent grammar for reading and understanding pictures in picture books' (2006: 4) and that the thesis of his book concentrates on the visual aspect of picture books, whereas their approach explores a 'variety of text–image interactions' (2006: 26) and the collaboration of words and pictures. Both books are informative and excellent in their own ways and as bookends they prop up a vibrant and crucial critical debate. However, there is an immediate sense of something missing in both studies, which is the child. And the issue of the child in relation to adult-produced, *child-centred discourse*, such as picture books, needs to be rehearsed a little here so that the following pages can be put into context. And, indeed, central to the ideas about to be explored is the child and a new way of seeing.

Nodelman describes picture books thus:

> Picture books – books intended for young children which communicate information or tell stories through a series of many pictures combined with relatively slight texts or no texts at all – are unlike any other form of verbal or visual art. Both the pictures and the texts in these books are different from and communicate differently from pictures and texts in other circumstances.
>
> (Nodelman 1988: vii, Preface)

In his extremely informative and useful study, Nodelman concentrates on this idea of the 'pictures' and the 'text' and indeed the combinations in relation to visual and verbal literacy development and how the reading child responds. This makes sense, of course, especially in the detached way of the critic who is self-consciously addressing the text alongside its means of delivery. Much research on early readers and picture books concentrate on the critical aspects of cognitive experience and on the differences and comparisons on reading the picture and reading the words as Nodelman reveals.

Indeed, Nikolajeva and Scott take a similar stance when they introduced their book on picture books by saying,

> The unique character of picturebooks as an artform is based on the combination of two levels of communication, the visual one and the verbal. Making use of semiotic terminology we can say that picture books communicate by means of two separate sets of signs, the iconic and the conventional.
>
> (Nikolajeva and Scott 2006: 1)

And of course they are right in identifying these two important levels of communication. But, as with Nodelman, they have actually missed the third and most important and unique component in the communication combination, in which the picture book and the early read to/reader are part and I think crucial to the entire verbal and visual experience. Nodelman alludes to it by saying,

> Young children who look at the picture while they listen to the words being read to them do experience both at once; but unlike the voices which emanate directly from the actors on stage or screen, the voice speaking a picture-book text remains separate from the visual information, a distinct stream of a noticeably different sort of information.
>
> (1988: viii)

But I have a problem agreeing with the main thrust of this and indeed with Nikolajeva and Scott's 'combination of two levels of communication'. What both of these quotations imply is that a picture book is a combination of text and image with a disembodied voice – principally and at least initially because they are designed to be read out loud by an adult/parent/teacher/older sibling etc. to a young child at the pre-reading stage. To some extent this is so, and the book doesn't speak like a television but, and this is incredibly important, there is a third (to add to the numbers game) and most important component.

There are three, not two 'levels of communication'. The third is the one of nurture, of shared experience, the relationship between the reader and the child as mediated by the book and the connections are explored and nurtured. It is as close as we can get to a critical, visual, literary and literal hug and to miss this point is to miss the function of the book and the potential it has in the nurturing process, and in making connections which Phillips referred to above. Throughout this book, I will keep repeating this third component is the combined intimacy, experience and connections that are being explored. And the idea of intimacy is so crucial to this.

For Deleuze, according to Colebrook (2002: 14), 'there is a direct link between philosophy, literature and ethics. If we limit thought to simple acts of representation – "this is a chair", "this is a table" – then we impose all sorts of dogmas and rules upon thinking.' Indeed, even from a critical perspective we need to read the whole picture not just the represented one. But we also need to think what we are introducing the child to in this moment of nurtured exploration. As Deleuze also indicated:

Everyday moral narratives, such as fables, parables and soap operas, operate with the fixed terms of good and evil, and so from a shared point of view of common sense and human recognition. Literature destroys this border between perceiver and perceived. We are no longer placed in a position of ordering judgement but become other through a confrontation with the forces that compose us. This is freedom: not a freedom to judge which comes from knowing who we are, but a liberation from our finite self-images, an opening to life. At its simplest level we can see how ethical becoming or freedom is limited by a fixed image of thought.

(Colebrook 2002: 131)

The picture book isn't just a book of stories and pictures; it is a vital part of much more physical, emotional and developmental discourse, which becomes a polysensory event, where all the senses of touch, sound, sight, smell and taste, story, warmth, security, affection and love can be brought together in the shared intimate experience of a story as nurture that is mediated by the book. As Webb and I have already written,

This involves several epistemological acknowledgements. One is to confirm that we are indeed dependent upon intimacy, and that it is incumbent upon us all to nurture such relationships. This is at the heart of the African philosophy of the self, *ubuntu*, the humanistic ideal that can be loosely translated as, 'a person is only a person in relation to others'. It is also at the heart of the communicative mode known as parrhesia: free speech, or openness; the speech that is about intimacy, honesty and truth. Intimacy is about communication with the other, and parrhesia is a form of intimacy that requires courage because there is risk involved in it: the risk of offending those to whom we are attached, the risk of hurting those we love, or those who love us, the risk of damaging our own reputation (Foucault 2001: 15–160).[1]

(Melrose and Webb 2011)

Not putting too fine a point on this, it is not just a muddle of words and images of representation in translation or interpretation, there is a huge emotive element to be considered. Of course this also goes beyond the book in the rituals of parenting and aspects of teaching and so on. There is not enough space to consider this here, and it is enough to say what I have in drawing attention to it. It is also an introduction into the whole wide world of ideas; the picture book is not just dealing with cognitive and intellectual development but the 'affective' which has to do with feeling and sensory experience. As I have written before,

This is nurture in action; this is experience in the making; this is about making the connections. I am even tempted to comment that never again in our lifetime will the relationship between adult and child ever get better than this – although this is not my field of expertise.

(Melrose 2002: 93)

In a reciprocal, shared experience the book becomes the mediator, as in this simple diagram, which I have shown in a previous book (Melrose 2002):

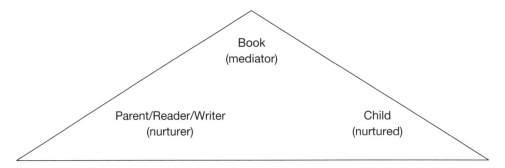

As mediator in an experience shared by both adult and child the book is a huge and important psychological and sociological tool. Rather than thinking of this as a diagram, think about it as an actual experience, think about it being a reader/parent (for example) on a sofa with an arm around the child while both of them engage with the book, one reading, the other looking at the pictures, listening to the words and engaging with the story.[2] But there is more to this, is there not? More in the affective moment of intimacy, in the closeness of the hearbeats and in the experience such moments engender. How can this have no bearing on the entire experiential process?

As I mentioned before, Walter Benjamin might have referred to this as the embodiment of the trading of experiences, the *Erfahrung*, where the shift between 'lived through' and 'narratable experience' is seen as a point of arbitration and negotiation, as an exploration of ideas, but this critical detachment gets nowhere near the sheer energy of such a moment.

While children may view the world from a different viewpoint to their adult counter-parts, as defined by age and experience, the astonishment and amazement at witnessing or hearing about the ongoing experience of sheer existence is the defining challenge at the meeting in the space in-between for both of them. And the adult has to be able to see this prospect in the child, who arrives on the proverbial knee to see the space in-between them being mediated by the wonder of storytelling. The book, the text, the story, the *objet d'art* stands as the mediator, as an arrested moment in experiencing something new which will not stand still, for it will never be new again, but will always be, Penelope-like,[3] starting over. Just as it did for the writer, so too will it for the reader. The arrested moment, the meeting between writer and reader, in that brief intercession, is the point at which ongoing experience is confronted just as it is about to move on.

Indeed, for the writer and reader for children this is not just arrested time, the time of our writing and reading, but the time at which we try to rationalise our internal struggles and strategies as well as those which exist outside to influence the historical moment of our writing, as reconstructed by our writing. To paraphrase Fredric Jameson's words, we are dealing with its ideological subtext so that it can be shared by the reader and the child (in a read to format) (1981). This seems to be so obvious but is missing from so much critical material on the (im)possibility of child-centred discourse. It needs to be hammered home, otherwise the child in the discourse remains hidden and mute and sidelined. Especially for early years children, the picture-book maker is helping to provide the story which allows them to explore and experience that nurture moment, as they come to reaffirm what they know and to try and understand what they know not. And let's not be coy, there is a definite reciprocal learning process going on here.

Phillips has already written on this when he says that, 'adults are not fully competent with their own instruments, but there is nobody else for the child to appeal to. Children go on asking, of course, but eventually they have to settle for the adult's exhausted impatience, and the *fictions of life*' (Phillips 1995: 1). But it's when Phillips goes on to qualify this that it becomes useful to the writer for children. He says, children's questions, 'just like the answers, can be baffling', going on to add, 'in *The Interpretation of Dreams*, Freud wrote, "nothing can be brought to an end, nothing is past or forgotten". Curiosity is endless . . . in a way that answers are not' (Phillips 1995: 1). And I love that idea of endless curiosity, constantly seeking answers. I might have it tattooed on my arm or at least pinned on my board as I write. But this is where the writer, the artist, the cultural practitioner has to step into the space between by providing a text that tells the reader who and what people are, what it is to live a life and what life can and is supposed to look like, what the artist does is make 'connections between curiosity and nurture' (Phillips 1995: 2) through storytelling, where 'ideally childhood is a series of reciprocal accommo-dations (or 'attunements' as they are now often referred to in an uneasy mixing of analogies)' (Phillips 1995: 4). The interaction taking place here is the ongoing negotiation of life itself, constantly curious for answers, constantly exploring the connections.

Thus the real unique character of picture books as an artform is based on the com-bination of three levels of communication, not two; the visual, the verbal and the socio/physiological as *affective* nurture. The third component is not some disembodied voice but the mutual exploration of the in-between space mediated by the text and confirming an experiential trinity. We could go further to say that with the best will in the world, the best story with the best illustration is nothing without the third component in the formative years. But get all three working together and the early 'exploration of the connections' are off to the best possible start. What the writer, artist, cultural practitioner does is help to make 'connections between curiosity and nurture' through the story narrative they are presenting, where ideally childhood is indeed a series of reciprocal accommodations. But in delivering the story in picture-book form the critic needs to be aware of his or her role in recognising the nurturing process. And I return to Deleuze when he says, 'No theory can develop without eventually encountering a wall, and practice is necessary for piercing this wall' (Deleuze, in Foucault and Deleuze 1972: 2). So let's proceed by developing some thoughts behind this idea.

Chapter 3

Life in the distillery

Shaping and producing child-centred art and early years writing involves a process of distillation (as a Scotsman I would say that, wouldn't I?). It is the slow extraction of the essence that is the story from the mass of images, ideas, research and other material ingredients gathered to produce it. Because, to put it quite simply, a picture book (say) is not a little story, it's a big story told short and this is really crucial to grasp. Much has to be said and done in less than eight hundred words and thirty-two pages (a gold star for guessing why thirty-two pages[1]). And writing this book as a critical exposé of such a process, as a detailed critical exegesis, as an accompanying and justifying, critical narrative is not something that can just be bashed off because there is much to know. Every picture-book writer/illustrator I have ever met has said the same thing to me, which is that picture books are absolutely the hardest books to write. There is nothing simple about them because there are so many things to address in the cult and culture of childhood if the art produced is to have an engaging presence and is fit for purpose.

Inevitably, therefore, whilst a critical narrative such as this book is a reflexive rationale behind the creative activity, it too is distilled from the research undertaken and the ideas collected in the creation of thoughts on the creative story to become a precise and concise validation, outlining the findings and supporting the justified decisions in the making process. However, what makes the particular rationale of picture-book making more complex than a simple, critical exposition of the creative process is the nature of the piece as art itself. Being a little hard on Nodelman, Nikolajeva and Scott earlier came about from my considering a different kind of commitment to this process from theirs; it came from ideas on the critically creative and creatively critical that I feel should enter the lexicon of research into picture books, and for good reason.

I don't just take a critic's eye view of this because for me a picture book is not just a stand alone, artistic exemplar. It has a function beyond its artistic definition, a *raison d'être*, which is that it is designed to serve as a means of mediating the experiential gaps in a child's life as he or she learns to grow into understanding. As explained above too, it is almost organic in its umbilical-like ability to (re)engage the parent/adult/teacher/reader with the child where the connections between stories and experience are explored. And to (re)engage and agree with Deleuze, the polysensory nature of the event of coming to the book is extremely important.

In some ways, it is easy to agree with Walter Benjamin when he wrote, 'Familiar though his name may be to us, the storyteller in his living immediacy is by no means a present force. He has already become something remote from us and something that is getting even more distant' (Benjamin 1973: 83). His words were prophetic when they were originally written in 1936 and still haunt us in the twenty-first century when we can see this is only the emergent age of internet technology and already the parameters are expanding day by day. Goodness, people I know read books on a machine with no pages, just a screen. And it doesn't just store one book but thousands of them. Who could credit all the millions of words and thousands of stories in an extensive library being stored on the back of an A5 envelope shaped machine?

Jack Zipes, too, shares Benjamin's pessimism when he writes,

> it is impossible to discuss the nature of storytelling today without talking about the global neglect of truth and authenticity. It is also frustrating and exasperating to talk about storytelling in our contemporary world in any kind of general way because of the immense diversity and complexity of storytelling, and because the truth claims about where the heart of storytelling lies and what storytelling is are often fallacious, deceitful, nefarious and ignorant. Even those sincere and inspired endeavours to extol and explore . . . is grossly obfuscated.
>
> (Zipes 2009: 142)

Heady words and thought provoking; however, when Benjamin went on to say, 'the art of storytelling is coming to an end . . .', which Zipes also addresses throughout his research, and which indeed is the subject of much postmodern anxiety, he entered a different debate and I feel this doomsaying rhetoric needs to be reconsidered. Think of it as a glass half full, rather than a glass half empty, to use a clapped-out old metaphor.

Not each and every example of picture book, early years story book, stage play, cultural event or film produced for children can have the interest of the child at heart. This is a fact of capital and consumerism which cannot be denied. I remember my own experience of sitting through a Disney Corporation video called *Detective Tigger*. As I have written elsewhere (Melrose 2001) the film is framed in false authenticity by being wrapped up in the 'ever same' timelessness of A. A. Milne's *Winnie the Pooh* stories, which have entered that hinterland of 'classic' stories for children: where the nostalgic longing for a return to an age when there was little else to choose from (this is a matter for another book) merely cheapens the worth of the term 'classic', which in any case is always an adult definition and as slippery as time itself. Despite the idea that nostalgia is the ultimate in displacement, a return to a time that never was, in a place the never existed, robbing the 'classic' of its clothing and re-presenting it to the contemporary is, indeed, classic. It is the emperor's new clothes and a classic postmodern trick which Disney has been perpetuating for decades.

In *Detective Tigger*, there is an episode called *Tigger, Private Ear* and I have no qualms in saying that in this little film Disney takes the commodification of story to new depths of concern. The story, like the emperor's new clothes, is, at worst, nakedly exploitative, and while showing some understanding of its intended audience, it pays little regard to that audience. The title of the film delivers the first indication of the crisis: *Tigger, Private Ear*. What is a 'private ear' for a child?

I am now old enough and sufficiently down the educational road of experience to understand wordplay, spoonerisms, malapropos, parody, irony and so on. So as the film proceeds I can deduce that 'private ear' is really meant to be a word play on 'private eye'. Indeed, it also plays on the character Tigger's tendency to get words wrong. This mannerism is fair enough. Tigger itself is a clearly a play on the word tiger. But tigger/tiger is an obvious image.

But where this idea in the script and images being presented comes unstuck is when a child is being expected to know what is really being meant, when they don't understand the root of the image being presented. Political satire works that way, does it not? If you are making satirical comment the joke is lost if the original idea hasn't been understood. At no time did the producers of this little film ask how many children aged four to seven, the film's target audience, would know what a private eye was, far less having to receive it displaced as a private ear? The whole concept of a 'private eye' is alien to their experience.

But it just gets worse. *Tigger, Private Ear*, opens to reveal a tall shadowy figure whom I recognise as a Sherlock Holmes character. He is wearing a cape coat, a deerstalker hat and carrying a pipe and magnifying glass. Indeed, he is not only Sherlock Holmes: he is Basil Rathbone's Holmes. And, further, the opening sequence moves into a Sherlock Holmesian routine, where the shadowy figure is looking for the 'Glockenspiel diamond'.

This carries on. 'Who shwiped the diamond?' asked Tigger. 'Was it the butler?' asked Pooh. But how is a child supposed to get any of these cultural references? Do they even know what a diamond is worth and who or what a butler is, far less the melodramatic idea that it was (always) the butler who stole the diamond? I doubt it.

All of these images, Rathbone's Holmes (as constructed by his clothes, pipe and magnifying glass – sorry no cocaine), the diamond (as booty), the butler (thief), are references which tug at the historical horizon of the televisually and literary experienced adult. I could go on at huge length about this but there is little point except to ask: at what age in your development do you think you would know what a 'superior sleuth' was? I had never come across the word 'sleuth' until I saw the 1972 film, directed by Joseph L. Mankiewicz, starring Laurence Olivier and Michael Caine, and I wasn't aged four then. The truth is such films are a simple device to 'hook children as consumers not because they believe their films have artistic merit and contribute to children's cultural development, but because they wanted to control children's aesthetic interests and consumer tastes' (Zipes 1997: 91) and it is sad and often true.

But thinking glass half full (we are in the distillery chapter after all), at least if we as critics and practitioners are aware of the creative and critical rationale we can help to try and engender greater care and attention in what is being produced. Story is about originality not the banal rehashing of the Disney project I just described. Art is not an indulgence; art is about saying something new, something vibrant and vital. As Hannah Arendt has argued, 'The chief characteristic of the specifically human life . . . is that it is always full of events that ultimately can be told as a story' (Arendt 1958: 72). I would extend this beyond 'events' to ideas and the Proustian idea of 'philosophic riches' that the story contains. But in response to Zipes' constant despair on this I am with Bertolt Brecht who adds to the story debate by saying, 'Reality changes; in order to represent it, modes of representation must also change. Nothing comes from nothing; the new comes from the old, but that is why it is new' (Brecht 1977: 81).[2] It is a constant battle but we have to wage it. Although it is necessary to add, it is not that art can't be fun. It patently can, and often needs to be where children are concerned, 'But art is, particularly at historical moments when many social values are under assault, a site in which questions of ethics and ontology and identity can be played out, and its function as this site is [all too often] being denied by voices of [adult] authority' (Webb 2005).

A picture book is many things, both an artefact and a literacy tool; an umbilical of nurture and a cultural and emotional experience. It almost seems crazy to suggest it but in a perfect world the child would go from womb to breast/bottle to picture book and onwards. Indeed when I said a picture book is a polysensory event, where all the senses of touch, sound, sight, smell and taste, story, warmth, security, affection and love can be brought together in the shared experience of a story as nurture that is mediated by the book, I can remember my daughter feeding on her last bottle of the day as I read *The Gruffalo*, 'A gruffalo? What's a gruffalo?' 'A gruffalo! Why, didn't you know? He has terrible tusks, and terrible claws, and terrible teeth in his terrible . . .' (Donaldson and Scheffler 1999). Many issues combine to produce the reflexive story, which exists beyond the straight artistic exercise, which is, itself, dependent on a whole raft of ideas and knowledge. But we must keep other factors in focus too. As Philip Pullman (1996) has said, 'We still need joy and delight, the promise of connection with something beyond ourselves. Perhaps children's literature is the last forum left for such a project.' Once again, these are not just wee stories, they are ginormous; so it's time to leave the distillery (sigh) and go looking for the child in the child-centred discourse.

Chapter 4

Know the child

What is clear is that while the book may be small and the story big, the child recipient of the picture book is small with a huge and quick learning brain. If you think about it, a child learns more in their formative years than they will in the long live happily ever after of the rest of their life – think about the stages between birth through eating, talking, walking, singing and dinosaurs (which came after *Thomas the Tank Engine* in our house). They go through many stages in reaching the picture book age. Let's consider this.

Children are born without language, without the means of differentiating signs and symbols, words and meaning. As Webb says, 'Nothing "means"; everything just "is"'. Of course none of us can remember this stage but at some point in our lives we have been and seen it. Slowly, the child is able to attach sense to the comings and goings around him or her:

> . . . she is not considered capable enough to be allowed to vote or enter into commercial contracts. She is what philosophers call the *chora*: a kind of third space or, in Derrida's interpretation of Plato, a 'halfway place, or 'half place' (Derrida 1995a: 116) . . . and for her too, the world is a chora: no longer a mass of undifferentiated signs, but not yet the organized and knowable world of the full symbolic subject.
>
> (Webb 2009: 67)

But even at this stage of development we can see how the cult and culture of childhood enters the marketplace. McLaren make racing cars and Maclaren make baby buggies but they must be in cahoots as high street shoppers dodge them racing around the corners. The commoditisation of the image of the cult and culture of the child and childhood, targeted at parents for children, starts very early indeed. Indeed, today, as I write, I am reminded that you can clothe your infant in a *Hungry Caterpillar* sleep suit and quite clearly research on parents reading the needs of their own infants might be fruitful.

The child, in the meantime, is leaving the *chora* and approaching what Lacan identifies as the mirror phase of their life. It becomes a world of meaning and signs being recognised. Curiously, the moment a child recognises itself in the mirror, at the time when it can say 'that's me' everything changes. 'The very act of recognizing her [his] image in the glass requires a distancing (That's me, over there [in the mirror]) and necessarily produces a split in her [his] sense of self – in her subjectivity' (Lacan 1997a: 188). (See Webb 2009: 67–8) 'From then on she [he] will know herself *as* herself – and me and only me, different from everyone and everything else'.) As Deleuze puts it:

how do I know I am me, and not you? Because I perceive a difference; because the things I conceive, imagine, remember, are mine and not yours; because I compare 'me' with 'you', and come up with a difference, with a space between us.

(Deleuze 1994: 137–8)

And there we see it, in this extraordinarily simple explanation, the 'in-between' space manifestly appears, normalised and immediately the site of nurture and exploration to be negotiated. This is not just an adult/child idea but that which exists between us all, between you and me as writer and reader, artist and reviewer, and so on, where you are not a passive observer but an active participator in the cultural event, whether it be reading or viewing and so on. I have written of this before:

In becoming, we necessarily acquire the phantasy that an 'I' exists, with discrete edges, with intrinsic difference from everyone and everything else; and yet we constantly run up against evidences that we are not much more than fragments in a larger story.

(Melrose and Webb 2011)

I will deal with the 'fragments' in a larger story idea later, but as a side issue, I urge you to think about this following idea seriously because it is about thinking as an artist. When you read this paragraph, stop to ponder: we are both meeting at the space in-between us. I write assuming you will come with prior knowledge and hoping to offer you something new, and assuming you will read with prior knowledge in the hope I have something more to offer. And yet my thinking of you (my reader) means I am trying to engage with you and mediate the space between us for our mutual benefit. In trying to figure out what you need in relation to what you want insists on my researching more and more to keep abreast. So your need to know makes me push the limits of my own knowledge in trying to provide it. Nothing changes that much from infancy onwards in this respect. Think of your own art like this when you are thinking about producing child-centred culture.

Crucial to this idea of the mirror stage for the child, though, is at the moment of knowing ourselves he/she is met with the moment of discovering 'lack'. To say 'I am me' is met with the representation of me in the mirror and in child-centred images that represent a child and childhood. 'In achieving my symbolic and divided self, I lose the connectedness of me' (Webb 2009: 69). There is a second loss too, that of full connection with all the things of the world. Finding out the world is not all about you and everything you experience is the world moves us away from that oneness of the self in acknowledging others, to one of knowing that from this stage on life is a negotiation between the self and the world, and between the real as experience and the real as represented vicariously.

Therefore, when something like a picture book comes into the field of vision of a child, the child comes to it knowing much already but looking at a representation of what it knows not. Go back to the Socratic idea discussed above. The book as mediator in child development is not so much explaining or showing but helping the child to connect to what they already know from other parts of life and then allowing them to take the ideas forward into something they may or may not have thought about but are ready to explore. The child will take the story you have offered and incorporate it with their own thinking to take possession of the knowledge the mutual exploration imparts. It is nurture in progress, 'because I compare "me" with "you", and come up with a difference, with a space between us . . .' (Deleuze 1994: 137–8), a space in-between being mediated by 'story', simple and uncomplicated, if you are producing story: whether it be oral, print, televisual, etc., it is a cultural event and you are mediating the site of exploration.

Chapter 5

The language of words, images and (in)completeness

In developing ideas on the picture book to be read for a child and for the emergent reader, one of the first things we need to analyse is how the picture book works as a textual blend of words and images in a 'nurturing' and a 'making the connections' process. We tend to think there has never been an age when images have not dominated our lives and that this is particularly so in this advanced age of advertising, television and internet technology. But language is much more complex than simply assuming our world is image-led. Everything in the process contributes to the 'story'. Of course, as Jack Zipes was to say, this is something we really need to be aware of:

> A child born at the beginning of the twenty-first century in America [and I would add, worldwide], no matter what class, color, or gender, has already been bombarded with messages and texts through design, electronics, and print by icons, signs, and sounds that come from adults, clothing, television screens, the radio, the movie screens, toys, games, and books . . . McDonalds has often had special gifts for children emanating from the Disney corporation or designs on their cups to lure children into their parlors.
>
> (Zipes 2009: 12)

I know these things, as a father I have witnessed them and bought into the toys; it is hard not to when you leave the cinema after having seen the new children's film – or should that be product, as Zipes might say? But as Sendak has said, children are 'intuitively aware'. It would be a mistake to think that children cannot differentiate between the vicarious and the real, between the product and real life and between product and real story. Sure my son dressed as Spiderman and acted out the scenes, but he never actually thought he was Spiderman, it was only a temporary phase of play. And when I see him now as a balanced and (as I write) interesting and interested, articulate and handsome sixteen-year-old, I can see how he has grown into maturity. His iPad does not dominate his life, though he does like having it around and the first thing he downloaded was an e-copy of *A Christmas Carol* by Charles Dickens, saying 'because I have never actually read the original'.[1] Just because information language comes at us from all over, it doesn't mean we cannot sift out the authentic from the white noise of technology.[2] Indeed, this takes us right back to the Brecht quotation, 'Reality changes; in order to represent it, modes of representation must also change. Nothing comes from nothing; the new comes from the old, but that is why it is new' (Brecht 1977: 81). Reading is already transferred into electronic form via the iPad and the Kindle but that doesn't mean to say story doesn't manage its ongoing fight for survival.

Indeed, if anyone had said even five or six years ago that I could watch you, the reader, reading this book, having downloaded it on to a five-inch machine while sitting hundreds of miles away, in another country even, I would have thought you mad. But a video call through Skype or a click on Google Earth could allow me to do just that. In fact if you find a Google location can you email me with a date and a time so I can wave to you. But to be fair, this would only be a distorted representation of the event of your reading. As Webb writes,

> A central issue in representation is that of substitution: it is widely understood as the process of standing in for someone or something, or acting as a substitute for the 'real thing'. A female character in a movie is seen to *stand in for* women everywhere; the words someone uses to tell their story *stand in for* the neurological processes that structure communication.
>
> (Webb 2009: 2–3)

And, indeed, this tells us a lot about the language of words and images in picture books and writing. But even knowing the picture book and story being represented is not really real, this 'standing in' need not remove the tenure of authenticity.

As we have seen in material from critics such as Nodelman, Nikolajeva and Scott, there is an inherent assumption that the picture book delivers its story through a developing understanding which combines image and text, and that the child's experience of story is enhanced in the process. As Bader states,

> A picture book is illustrations, total design; an item of manufacture and a commercial product; a social, cultural, historical document; and, foremost, an *experience* for a child. As an art form it hinges on the interdependence of pictures and words, on the simultaneous display of two facing pages, and on the drama of the turning of the page. On its own terms its possibilities are limitless [my italics].
>
> (Bader 1976: 1)

Picking up on this use of the word 'experience' here, the experience presented is only part of the exercise and to overplay this idea is to lose sight of experience itself, the development of cognitive understanding in allowing a child exposure to stories which become part of their own, as yet to be articulated, story that is their life in action.

The child's involvement in the picture book as a read to/reading process is one of exploring which is crucial to the developing life experience, which for all of us is partly lived and partly vicarious. I stated previously (Melrose 2002: 92) that, 'picture books can help develop the difference between reading words and reading pictures', supporting the argument of Peter Hunt (1991: 175–88). But I now realise there is much a larger issue to be explored here. Stewig (1995: 9) has written that the words and images cannot ultimately be seen as two separate forms in the picture book but should be perceived as a whole narrative, a story in completeness where one cannot work without the other. I can see how the critical underpinning of this works but the problem is that it takes the picture book as a stand-alone artefact and it is not quite as simple as this. And, indeed, the idea of anything being a story in completeness troubles me and I think it is important to unpick this a little. As I have also written elsewhere,

> The idea that a representation of reality, created in any form, such as a novel or a film, for example, could be transferred from the real to the represented without change is a fantasy. It is a representation never a precise replication. The representation is in itself an experience, but it does not replace the true experience, it merely sits alongside it as another experience. The book [film, play, artistic event] is the medium through which the writer's experience is translated into a story. Thus, it mediates the transference of the experience of the writer to the reader as another experience.
>
> (Melrose 2002: 9)

What it is not and can never be is a whole narrative. No story in a book is 'complete'; it is a 'representation' to accompany other representations alongside the real, and as such is only a component part of a much wider experience which is the story narrative. The book doesn't provide completeness in the story, it opens up possibilities. The receiver, the reader, the child all bring ideas to the text which are huge contributing factors. None of us are read to or read passively, none of us attend a stage play passively, view an artwork passively: it is an active, cultural event. In the case of a young child and to repeat (again) it is an event where all the senses of touch, sound, sight, smell and taste, story, warmth, security, affection and love can be brought together alongside historical learning and the astonishment of the new in the shared experience of a story as part of the nurturing process. And while Nodelman spent great swathes of his book *The Hidden Adult: Defining Children's Literature* on the idea of 'the hidden adult' in childrens' literature, which he concludes by saying, 'Children's literature is literature that claims to be devoid of adult content that nevertheless lurks within it' (Nodelman 2008: 341), I can't help repeating that, for me, the adult in children's cultural product is not hidden but the biggest elephant in the room and that the person critics should be focused on is the 'hidden child'. We need to get the message home that the picture book, the film, the play is part of a much wider cultural narrative system and storehouse of the child and childhood, and much larger than the simple issue of the (in)completeness of words and pictures on a page.

It might be useful to think of the cultural experience and the narrative storehouse as a *Wunderkammer*. As Webb says, 'Of course the notion that it is primarily artists who reflect on and make representations about society is too limiting; engagement with, critique of and reflections on society, and the translation of such reflections into representations, is very much a human act' (Webb 2005). Children are an inexhaustible receptacle of story narrative where they gather the fragments, souvenirs, memorabilia, photographs, images, words, ideas, thoughts, dreams, hopes and desires as their own personal collection of incomplete narratives that go to make up their understanding of the self. In their own little and ever expanding *Wunderkammer* they put on record their own and others' stories.

> This is both a valid and a necessary act: 'art' (or making representations) in this broadest sense, as well as in the more commonly accepted sense of 'art,' is about keeping the soul alive: it involves our being human, telling stories, and crafting, critiquing and maintaining society. It demands responsibility in the selection of stories to be told, and in the selection of perspectives from which to do the telling.
>
> (Webb 2005)

In thinking about the child as a *Wunderkammer*, of course, I am not describing him or her as a cabinet of curiosities, or a cabinet of wonder, but I am using it as a metaphor for the child, not as some structural and structuralist repository but as a bottomless storehouse of story narrative. In which case, to use the same terminology, he and she are the *Wunderkinder*.

Historically, a *Wunderkammer* was supposed to have displayed examples of 'strange' things from the natural world, the newest discoveries in zoology, geology, etc., as well as extraordinary objects made by human hands, but also those objects from the 'other' natural world so-called, such as basilisks' fangs, unicorns' horns, mermaids' spines and dragons' teeth, and we can see how it comes to be represented textually in story form. The Harry Potter novels are literal *Wunderkammern*, full of such combinations of muggle and magical objects and artefacts, such as a Ford Anglia, a deluminator, an invisibility cloak and a sorting hat; along with corporeal creatures, like the animagus, patronus, boggarts, dementors and thestrals for example. But there is something persuasive in its metaphorical potential as an explanation of a repository of experiences as story that is the *Wunderkind/* child, which combines the real and the imagined and the self and other. Is this not closer to a description of the (in)complete story narrative of the child and childhood?

But that is not to say the picture book does not have a huge part to play as a story narrative. As Webb also says,

> One strand of this loop is the fact that there is little actual difference between the experience of physical stimuli, and the mental abstraction of reading and thought. This might seem unlikely; but . . . the gap between the 'real world' and 'mere representation' is not always as evident as common-sense would suggest. New research into how the brain works is shifting our understanding of how individuals make sense of the world, and convey sense to others . . . representation is considerably more than a simple matter of standing in for; it is also productive of what we know, and how we know it: that is to say, it is communicative – it makes us.
>
> (Webb 2009: 5)

And this idea of it being 'productive of what we know, and how we know it: that is to say, it is communicative – it makes us' is extremely relelvant and interesting. We can immediately see how the in-between space can be negotiated to great and responsible effect, where the cultural event like the picture book becomes this force of good in the cognitive, experiential and social development of the child, just at the moment when the child is trying make sense of the world. Stories, after all, function to help us understand who we are, where we have been, and where we might be going.

I do feel we need to pin this idea down. When I say that both the child and the adult are exploring the boundaries of experience in the space in-between, I am not just suggesting that the adult can teach the child to tie their shoelaces. It is much more fundamental than that because it is life itself that is being explored, not just particular topics of knowledge. I have rehearsed this debate at greater length in *Here Comes the Bogeyman* but it needs to be contextualised a little here.

It is impossible, I suspect, to propose a non-exclusionist normative definition of textual engagement in writing for children and in entering this space in-between, but surely a normative structure that clarifies the intrinsic distinctiveness of child-centred storytelling can be proposed? As writers we need to be aware of the kind of cultural exclusion/

inclusion ideas involved in this exploration process for it seems to me it is recognisable by looking at the idea of 'normative' in three ways and it will help if I isolate them a little.

The *first* is the Jacqueline Rose style, affirmation of the superiority of the adult over the child, which excludes the child from full participation in the discourse taking place in the space in-between. In thinking about it, it is a kind of denial of any free will as a 'do as I say' commandment which seems a rather unlikely scenario in the twenty-first century.

The *second* is more likely, in allowing participation of the child, but one where the adult dictates the normative rules without some kind of appreciation of what the child needs and wants. The reason being that mother, father, guardian, teacher, etc., knows better; which is itself problematised.

The *third* way (if indeed it is a way – I am only using the word as a means of expressing it) is about taking much more of a dialogic and vigilant approach to the idea of normative. The first two ideas and attitudes are embedded in dominant adult ideology, institutions and practices which have become normative in a hierarchical, symbolic framework of *child-centred discourse*, where the only qualification required of the expert is to be adult. But I would contend that adult practitioners, artists, writers, film-makers and the like, and thereby producers of child-centred culture, do not need a new way of seeing or being but simply need to maintain a state of constant vigilance in observing what is being done to and in the name of the child. Although rather than approaching this as a critic I would encourage writers and practitioners to look at ways of addressing the social and aesthetic transformation of the culture of writing for children. And this can be done by writing in such a way that your reader will see an approach to ideas, issues and 'aesthetics that could radically alter their way of reading' what the normative is.[3] In this way, writing for children could and indeed is a radical force for good when approached this way.

But to me the huge role the picture book can play in all of this lies in the element of surprise. And once again we have to take the critical subtext down to basic ideas, which is that child comes to understand representative story through surprise and through wanting to know what happens next. Of course a child may and indeed will return to the same book over and over, looking for new things each time but also because they are reassured by what surprised them previously and this is such a simple idea. I will repeat this so many times that it will become a mantra but it is that Socratic idea all over again. It's not so much explaining or showing but helping others to connect to what they already know from other parts of life and then asking them to take the ideas forward into something they may or may not have thought about but are ready to explore. The child will take the story you have offered and incorporate it with their own thinking to take possession of the knowledge the mutual exploration imparts – it is nurture in progress. But like everything else in their life they will come back and each day the expanded experience they bring can still revisit the old cultural site (in this case a book or a film) to be reassured by what they see but also to see what they might have missed and even to see what is new. It might be a new part of the story, or a new story in the continuing story of their life. Once again put yourself in their shoes: do you ever stop doing this even in adulthood?

Perry Nodelman's significant commentary on this issue of picture books is really useful on this and it is something we should all note. He suggests, 'a picture in a picture book confirms and makes more specific a story that is already implied by the context of previous and subsequent pictures' (1988: viii). And he is right. A random picture in a picture book stands in isolation but the story relies on the preceding and following pictures for clarity and maintaining the narrative thread. Even the movement from the front cover to the first story page has a context in this. There is little point in the text saying, 'We don't know he was called Moonlight' when the title of the book is *A Kitten Called Moonlight*, immediately giving the visual and verbal game away. But let's develop this idea because there are two strands to it which are useful to understand.

Firstly, the picture book experience is like real life experience in the context Nodelman gives. The picture page relies on the page before for context so that it can reveal the new and the promise of something newer to come on the page that follows. But think of this in terms of the child who come to the book, or the page in this case, with what they know already to that which they know not, each experience being a page-turning exercise in experience. One of the reasons children return to the same picture book time and time again is all about repeat experience which (re)confirms the familiar, that which they know, while being confronted minute by minute by the new.

The second is easier to examine because it is less abstract. I was in Australia recently and I didn't eschew the strange foods on display, I challenged my palate. I tested the water for new experiences. I am not saying whether I ate anything off this board, below, but put your imagination to the test and see what a child sees in an isolated picture book.[4] Take in as much information as you can.

Taking Nodelman's point, if this picture had been *preceded* by a picture of a field of kangaroos, deer, goats, crocodiles, emus, ostriches, possum, wild or white rabbits, hares, etc., and then *followed* by a table groaning with cuts of meat, would the image above have been quite so benign when seen as part of a wider narrative? Thus we can see how the pictures are rich narrative resources in storytelling (I don't know how game those animals were, by the way, but never mind the white rabbit or wild rabbit, I would be pretty wild if I were on this list – and isn't wordplay around words like 'game' and 'wild' an interesting game for child-centred discourse too).

Nodelman also makes the suggestion as to how words can add to the richness of this story because they communicate so differently from pictures but that also because they can change the meaning of pictures. I could write a narrative around this illustration that would render the board completely benign. Of course it might be a child's version of *Setting Free the Bears* (Irvine 1968) but even the title of this book, *Monsters Under the Bed*, gives a visual and verbal narrative image. Imagine, instead, in another reading of the story of the picture, what would it be like if it were followed by another picture book image of all of the animals escaping! All the kangaroos, deer, goats, crocodiles, emus, ostriches, possum, rabbits, wild white hares, etc., running amok in delightful chaos, instead of ending up as slabs of meat. What is clear is that pictures and words can change the narrative energy inherent in the story. Not just those on the single page or double spread but in the combination that comes before and after.

That a combination of pictures and words can actually come together to tell a story, even when the pictures and words are in conflict, can be a powerful tool. Advertising uses this technique a great deal. The 1994 Wonderbra[5] advertisement, featuring a picture of Eva Herzigova stripped down to her underwear beside a caption that said, 'Hello Boys', was voted the most iconic advert image of all time. I know, you are groaning and saying, how like a man to choose this advertisement, and I will spare you the picture, but there is something curiously interesting about an advert for a woman's product being targeted at men, or women who wish to please men, and it was immensely effective. This is not the place to go into the whole idea of truth and lies and ethical responsibility (which we are taking on trust here) but our understanding of language in image and text is crucial to this and indeed in the understanding is a clear view of how children can be exploited in a similar way.

We could spend years investigating this thing called 'language', as many such as Derrida and Wittgenstein have, but a concise description comes from Jen Webb when she says,

> Language works through a process that involves using signs to stand in for concrete objects or ideas. Signs include words (both written and spoken), gestures, architec-tural design, art works, musical notation and sounds, hair styles, dress, and any other range of the devices people use to connect one with another. Language is a repre-sentational system because it provides *something* to stand in for (to represent, to make present) *something else*.
>
> (2009: 40)

Think about this for just a moment, I am using words here, in writing this; actually if we analyse them as signs they are little more than squiggles on a page that we have learned to comprehend as a written form of language, but let's take a small sample of the 'signs' she refers to through the following questions and try to answer them yourself, so that you can imagine how difficult it will be for the quickly leaning child:

Words question: what does love feel like?

I am not being coy but I have no answer to this and I suspect there is no universal answer that would satisfy all readers. We have the five senses which we use to hear, see, smell, touch or taste, but what of the sense that makes us feel, for what sense records joy or pain or anger or love? And then there are the associates, desire, passion and so on, none of them a visual or a verbal expression; but these are all the elements we explore in stories and are elements the skilled writers and artists will have to address some time in their career, even in producing for early years children. But reduced to words alone it is problematic and I am reminded of Freud's description of kissing, which goes to show how language is often constrained by its own ability to describe. Is this the best kiss of your life?

> . . . the kiss . . . between the mucous membrane of the lips of the two people concerned, is held in high sexual esteem among many nations (including the most highly civilized ones), in spite of the fact that the parts of the body involved do not form part of the sexual apparatus but constitute the entrance to the digestive tract.
>
> (Freud 1983: 150)

I think we can leave it at that, you get what I mean.

Signs question: what does this mean?[6]

Simple, huh? Just imagine you have to direct your child reader to their new school toilet. I mean one of these picture people is confusing enough, although I am sure we get the idea pretty early on, even if they only just resemble female and male figures. I am Scottish (have I said that?) and I was once in a bar in my home town, Edinburgh. It was a theme bar, all horsey and brass and tackle and the toilet doors had signs that said the words 'Colts' and 'Fillies'. As I approached them an old friend of mine exited sheepishly from the wrong door; he had walked into the ladies. He said, in his broad Scottish accent, 'Ah huvnae got mah glasses on. I thought it said Fellies' (*n*. Scots vernacular, a fellow, man . . .).

Spoken words question: read this sign out loud, does it make you laugh?[7]

This sign is on the esplanade by the beach in my adopted home, Brighton, which has, in the past, had a British humour, naughty seaside reputation. And I have heard three separate, well-known comedians make a joke out of this. Even though it is a serious sign with a serious point to be made about falling in the sea, humour can be instilled by innuendo and double entendre to great effect.

Musical notation question: what do you think of when you see this?[8]

It is not a language I read too well although I do play a number of musical instruments; and rather it is a language I like to address by hearing, not reading, which is another cultural, sensory event. Of course, for those who cannot read it, it is Beethoven's Symphony No. 5.

Art works question: is it art or a functional display?[9]

What is art? I came across this table in a greengrocer's shop in Canberra and in its full colours of orange and green and brown it was such a wonderful pyramid and I was taken too by how the greengrocer had taken such pride in the art and craft of his display. But seeing this picture again reminds me of Chaco Kato's *Pulp Fiction*[10] polysensory exhibition.

It was described thus:

> It's the smell that hits you first. The fragrance of decomposing citrus and passion fruit and cantaloupe is hardly the kind of sensory experience you expect in a gallery setting. But wandering about the ornate installations of composting micro-sculptures and hanging, mobile-like arrangements that comprise artist Chaco Kato's *Pulp Fiction* exhibition at Craft Victoria smell isn't the only presumption to be tested. Many of us consider an art work in terms of a completed object – a kind of historical marker that lasts for decades, even centuries. But spending time with Kato's work reveals a space in transition.[11]

But if we took the picture above and matched it with this poem (below), which the exhibition does, the levels of engagement and representation shift in perspective. In engaging with Kato's work, Webb said,

> I started by thinking about change, and that led me to the Roman poet Ovid, who wrote a collection of poem/stories called *Metamorphoses*.

> Ovid, that old reprobate, he
>
> understood the processes of
>
> change
> How a boy might
>
> become a bird,
> or lovers be transformed
>
> into trees.
> You too know
>
> transformation – setting your
>
> own course
>
> the slow sifting, shifting
> from charcoal to jewel – a
>
> fugitive
> from function into form. An
>
> egg shell becomes
> Fabergé, melon seeds a
>
> string of gems,
> skin dries into a cord that
>
> holds the moment
>
> when everything changed,
>
> when falling became flight,
> discard changed to desire.
> There is a story behind every

skin; every
minor miracle, another

metamorphosis.
    (Webb 2009: 40)[12]

The evident relationship between images and words here is manifest. But in moving away from the literariness and idea of art coming out of discarded commodity we find the discourse wrestling with the cynical product working in a picture book medium; which, after my assessment, should not be purchased to be discarded.

> **Book question**: this week, as I write, sees the launch of a new illustrated book entitled *Go the F**k to Sleep* (Adam Mansbach and Ricardo Cortés 2011) – would you be able to ask for it in the bookshop?

Personally I find the concept of this hugely successful book a little nauseating. It is a picture book for adults. Not in the way of *Maus* by Art Spiegelman or something equally as interesting: it is just a joke. And OK, I can take a joke along with everyone else, but why would an adult purchase, sit down and then read a book with such a shallow sentiment? I can see who would purchase it, and indeed give it as a humorous gift, but like *Harry Potter and the Philosopher's Stone* with its 'for adults' cover, surely there are better things for adults to read? My personal recommendation of the day would be Philip Gross's *The Water Table* (a great writer for children and adults and winner of the 2009 T. S. Eliot Prize). But if it had to be a picture book I would much rather replace the *Go the . . .* book with Jill Murphy's wonderful story *Five Minutes' Peace*, which has a similar theme but says masses about children and adults needing time and space to explore. Or the monstrously wonderful story about parents too preoccupied to notice their own child, *Not Now Bernard* by David McKee.

> **Cultural question**: is this public health sign on a dance floor? I mean look at the jazz dancing hands on the man.[13]

OK, I confess, this one is just a bit of a joke which I found amusing, and I can share a joke, can't I? After all, some of these kinds of signs are funny when the context is removed or played with, which we can all do in the course of our lives. The artist Banksy does it as an art form and his *Kissing Policemen* in Brighton, where Gay Pride is held every year, is famous[14] (Google: Banksy Kissing Policemen – there are pictures all over[15]). But this kind of wordplay goes on all over the world. Near to where I live there is a village by the name of FULKING[16] and some wag is always changing the 'L' to a 'C'. I hear the council is thinking of installing CCTV to deter the prankster. Let them have their joke, I say.

The whole world is made up of signs and symbols and words like this on a page and spoken words and hidden thoughts and images and ideas, and endless ellipses . . . that just go on and on forever. But as Webb also reveals:

> [Language] . . . is not only representational. It also works as a system of reference because a word or other sign does not simply stand in for the thing, but also refers people to that thing. And it does more than this: language not only represents, refers or otherwise communicates aspects of the world. It also, according to most contemporary and many much earlier theorists, frames the world so that in particular ways the world becomes available to us.
>
> (Webb 2011)

Picture books fit into this framing as a system of reference, not as a didactic matter of instruction but a combined narrative that allows the child to explore the boundaries of their own knowledge, each bringing that which they know to that which they know not, as knowledge and experience expand in the continuous way that living provides. But they are also experiencing the language that will allow them to interpret and articulate their own evolving sense of self and other – and how crucial is that?

Children in the twenty-first century have many forms of text available to them and, as can be seen in the small and very simple sample above, we all have a huge variety which are ever-changing and indeed change the ways in which we, as well as young readers, are expected to read. Much of our learning is carried by images. Indeed, as I was asked the other day, which hope would I choose, Inner or Outer? The answer is in the endnote, so you have a choice whether to check or not.[17]

Thus, while suggesting that picture books use two signifying systems, words and pictures in fusion seems to be obvious to the creative process, it is way too simple because the social interaction is much greater than the sum of these two parts. Kress summarises it eloquently when he says,

> The shape of what there is to read has its effects on reading practices, and the understanding of what reading is. Both develop in the constant interaction between the shape of what there is to read, the socially located reader and their human nature.
>
> (Kress, cited in Styles, Bearne and Watson (eds) 1996: 137)

This idea of the 'the socially located reader and their human nature' cannot be removed from the equation. And I repeat what I have said earlier, the picture book isn't just a book of stories and pictures; it is a vital part of a much more physical, emotional and developmental discourse, which becomes a polysensory event, where all the senses of touch, sound, sight, smell and taste, story, warmth, security, affection and love etc. can be brought together in the shared experience of a story as nurture that is mediated by the book. I know I have said that a couple of times before but it should be worn like a lucky charm bracelet of critical underpinning. According to Jacques Lacan:

> One can only think of language as a network, a net over the entirety of things, over the totality of the real. It inscribes on the plane of the real this other plane, which we here call the plane of the symbolic.
>
> (Belsey 2005: 4)

Once again, from a purely practical point of view in developing this idea, picture-book makers have to consider what exactly best represents the story. Few of us will get the opportunity to actually design the book (unless we are writer illustrators) since for most picture books the written text is turned over to the publisher for illustration. But knowing about it helps our view of the discipline and indeed our view of the story and how it is shaped. Too much information in this process cannot be bad for the writer/maker.

In *Granpa* by John Burningham (1984), for example, the double-spread illustrations tell two stories from two different perspectives. The left-hand page is (mostly) in black and white and the right-hand page is in colour, which is significant. Firstly what we see is two stories being told simultaneously. Text-wise, the girl's story is told in italics (presuming dialogue from the child) and the Granpa's in a normal font. As Nikolajeva and Scott say of this double spread, 'The counterpoint between the dialogue, the line drawing, and the full colour picture [the right-hand picture is colour in the original] produces a multi-dimensional sense of the characters and their relationship.' And the picture is full of information, as they also go on to say,

> A good example [of the counterpoint] is the triad of dialogue, drawing, and picture that centers on games and sport. In the color spread, Granpa is playing with his granddaughter's skipping rope while she looks on from her bicycle with its training wheels . . . Granpa's beatific smile and closed eyes, shows us that he is really enjoying himself with the child's toy, and the dialogue let's us know that the play has brought back memories of his own boyhood: 'When I was a boy we used to roll our wooden hoops down the street after school.'
>
> (2006: 112)

In an overview of the story, the ageing Granpa is juxtaposed textually with his grand-daughter. At the same time as she is moving forward in her life story, he is reflecting on his past while his life story is in decline. And indeed we can see how the child in the text is trying to imagine her Granpa as a child though his retrospective stories. The whole idea is normalised by the idea of the beginning and the end of life – and there is no parent/daughter/adult to straddle the two stories as the Granpa's death is finally represented symbolically by a picture of an empty chair. And even a child can understand the meaning of loss and erasure being implied in the symbolism here. But, crucially, the child recipient of the story is able to absorb the vicarious experience for future reference. After all, isn't it just the most curious thing about living is that it always leads to death in the end (Oh! and taxes)?

I was thinking of this as an adult and two things came to the fore which the real and symbolic granddaughter would not be able to connect but will be able to in time. The first is from Sigmund Freud who wrote this on creativity:

> Should we not look for traces of imaginative activity as early as in childhood . . .? Might we not say that every child at play behaves like a creative writer, in that he creates a world of his own, or, rather, rearranges the things of his world in a new way, which pleases him. It would be wrong to think he does not take life seriously and he expends large amounts of emotion on it . . . The creative writer does the same as a child at play. He creates a world of fantasy which he takes very seriously – that is, which he invests with large amounts of emotion – while separating it sharply from reality. *Language has preserved this relationship between children's play and poetic creation* [my italics].
> (Freud 1990: 131–2)

I just think that this tiny book of illustration from Burningham says more about this than its immediate simplicity suggests and is an exemplary example of creative thinking. Though I am also alerted to this because it's a great message for the creative writer and thinker, unlike the other quotation that came to mind, 'When I was a child, I spake as a child, I understood as a child, I thought as a child: but when I became a man, I put away childish things' (King James Bible 1611: 1 Corinthians 13:11). This is the antithesis of everything I believe on the issue of writing for children, exploring the in-between space and the mutual march into experience as nurture.

But back to *Granpa*: Nikolajeva and Scott give a very good reading of this book (2006: 111–15) and there is too much to rehearse or even summarise here. But they also reveal an aspect of the book which I think is very crucial. They write:

> While it's perhaps dangerously academic to overinterpret the possibilities . . . what is certainly true is the degree of involvement demanded of the reader, not simply in interpreting what the book is conveying, but, because of the ambiguity, in empathizing with the characters and injecting elements of one's own emotions and experience into the work. In drawing the readers into the process of characterization, Burningham makes them feel like *participants in the relationship* he depicts [my italics].
> (Nikolajeva and Scott 2006: 235)

This is exactly what I meant when I referred to the participatory aspect of the text as a mediator. This text is perfect for that idea of participation: participants in the relationship between the grandchild and Granpa; participants in the story they represent; participants in the problem of ageing; participants in the extended symbolic meaning that the story can represent every child/granpa relationship. The picture book in this case is dealing with a universal truth in thirty-two simple pages. Not so much a little story as a huge one!

But this participatory idea doesn't always work. A picture book entitled *A Kitten Called Moonlight* (2000) by Martin Waddell and Christian Birmingham makes a huge effort to achieve this, but combined text and image idea becomes obfuscated by the combined complexity of the visuals and narrative voice being used. The book itself replicates the picture book experience because it features a mother and child relationship, where the mother and child are discussing a story they share but instead of making the reader (outside the book) a participant in the relationship being represented in the text we are made to feel like outsiders.

Here is a small extract which is self-explanatory and you need to note the speech marks because the book is a conversation between Charlotte and Mummy. What is essentially happening is the story is being refracted through two people talking about themselves in the third person, about when they were first involved in the story, and it is all terribly convoluted. Mummy is speaking (telling the story) and Charlotte is interrupting, simulating the picture book process inside an actual picture book – which means the actual reader and child is getting it third hand (if that makes sense).

> "The little girl . . . and her mummy went down
> to the shore. They searched and
> they searched but they couldn't
> find anything. 'Something *was*
> here,' said the little girl.
> "She knew she was right,"
> Charlotte said.

> "Yes," Mummy said. "But her
> Mummy wasn't sure. She said,
> 'We'll take one more look,
> Just in case.'"

(Waddell and Birmingham 2000)

I remember that Arthur Scargill, the then leader of the National Union of Mineworkers, used to speak about his own actions by referring to himself by name instead of using the first person pronoun 'I'. It is a very odd device which we really ought to not use. Speaking here for myself, Andrew says, 'Andrew Melrose does not speak of himself or his actions like this'. It's a bit affected and odd, and you can see how the Mummy and the girl Charlotte are talking in conversation about themselves and about each other in third person, in the present and in flashback/analepses, which does not generally work in picture books (Andrew will come back to this – oops – although curiously *Granpa* which I referred to above has a slight element of this to it). But when young children do this, they are only repeating a parental/carer/teacher dialogue affectation. We could rehearse it here: 'So,' Mummy was wondering, 'what did Tommy do today?' We have all heard children refer to themselves in this way too, 'Well, Tommy went to the seaside,' replied Tommy – it's all a bit of an affectation in real life and that is another reason why it doesn't work in a book.

But while *A Kitten Called Moonlight* is confusing, even for this reader, my own feeling is that while the book makes a great effort to tell a story (and the premise is a good one) it is difficult to use it as an inclusive text. In many ways it's a book about nurture which doesn't assist the parent/reader in the nurture process. This is because the child reader/child being read to is expected to do nothing but spectate as an outsider to the story, while the storyteller inside the book is talking to the daughter inside the book, while she, the 'inside' daughter, keeps interrupting the real story – and even my trying to explain it here has its own difficulties. It is, it has to be said, very unusual from Martin Waddell, who wrote the splendid (in my view) *Can't You Sleep Little Bear*, which is also a book about nurture and a 'child' interrupting an 'adult', but one which involves the reading/read to child. It was an idea with good intentions, which I will address in Part II.

Chapter 6

Counterpointing connections

I have mentioned Nikolajava and Scott's *How Picturebooks Work* before and do urge you to read around the wider critical debate they provide. They write, 'If words and images fill each other's pages wholly, there is nothing left for the reader's imagination, and the reader [child read to] remains somewhat passive' (2006: 17). This is exactly what I was saying above when I suggested that a picture book was a participatory piece of art which encourages engagement. And in thinking about the passivity problem they add,

> The same is true if the gaps are identical in words and images (or if there are no gaps at all). In the first case, we are dealing with the category named 'complementary,' in the second, 'symmetrical.' However as soon as words and images provide alternative information or contradict each other in some way, we have a variety of readings and interpretations.
>
> (2006: 17)

They then go on to discuss how counterpoints between the text and image manipulate a narrative tension. As Zipes comments,

> it is often through the ironic juxtaposition of word and image, word and word, and image and image that the reader becomes aware of incongruous and bizarre formations. Regardless of whether the reader is a child or an adult, the fantastic in picture books fails when it is merely descriptive, complementary, decorative, or titillating. It succeeds best when it provokes the reader to stand back, take a second look, doubt and reflect.
>
> (Zipes 2009: 57)

He is essentially talking about ideas on fantasy when he mentions fantastic fiction. But I would much rather take a less restrictive meaning of the word fantastic because these ideas affect all pictures books, which to all intents and purposes are fantastic stories. But I do have an issue when he goes on to add,

> Often image and text resist one another. The resistance to convey direct meaning and draw literal parallels with reality is at the heart of the design of picture books that make effective use of the fantastic to provide resistance to reality and that show how reality can be transformed.
>
> (Zipes 2009: 57)

I have no problem with the validity of this point but surely all pictures in picture books are counterpoint representations of true-to-life stories framed in fictional texts. Also, life is not a linear thread without interruption and the best picture books do reveal this in many different ways. Counterpoint, say Nikolajava and Scott, offers the reader alternative and often conflicting information, reaching out as far along the narrative scale from complementary to contradiction. And, as Zipes implies, this counterpoint idea makes us think, or as Webb says, 'representation is considerably more that a simple matter of standing in for; it is also productive of what we know, and how we know it: that is to say, it is communicative – it makes us' (Webb 2009: 5).

In its most basic form as discussed previously, this can be collected and collated under the heading of 'exploring the connections'. It really is that simple. Is this not something we all do in our lives, analysing and interpreting counterpointing narratives, images and words? Even in our sleep we are dealing with the conflicting narratives as dreams which often defy comprehension. But when a really good picture book like *Granpa* really comes together it can tell us a huge amount about story. But that is not the end of the story. Words themselves can survive without pictures, as they come to do later in our lives when we import our own thoughts and images into the narratives we read as adults. But I was thinking too about a picture book without words, the glorious *The Snowman* (Briggs 1978) because I have a personal story about that.

I worked for a time with the film director Jimmy Murakami, who worked on the animation film of the picture book. He was in my house one evening and we watched a bit of the film on television. When it got to the part when the boy and Snowman fly from the South Downs over Brighton, England (where I live) and over the Royal Pavilion and Palace Pier, Jimmy said to my son, Daniel, 'Look, they are flying right over your house.' And this is the case. If you ever see that clip of the film and if you take the route as the crow flies, my attic window is straight in line with the pier, which I can see every single night, glittering like a magic wand laid on a midnight blue, briny table. So what? you might be saying. Well, it's my story; you see the next time we watched the film, Daniel ran to the window to see if Snowman and the boy were really real and really there. It was a moment of *Erfahrung*, the moment where the story hovered between the 'lived through' and the 'narratable' experience and I am smiling now as I recollect it. What was great to see was the engagement with the picture book, the film and the oral story told by Jimmy, all combining in the imagination of a little boy who was exploring for himself – just like the story in the picture book itself. Of which Nodelman says,

> *The Snowman* is a worldless picture book. The fluidity of its style makes up for the lack of words – it implies variations in our relationship with the characters that create a specific sort of involvement with the action depicted. Obviously, the best way picture books can convey narrative information of that sort is . . . by using words. But the large number of picture books that contain no words at all raises important questions about how well pictures by themselves can depict events that we can recognize as stories.
>
> (Nodelman 1988: 185)

In a highly personalised account, Virginia Lowe makes a well-expressed appeal in urging adults to trust children's intelligence and sensitivity to appreciate the reality in a given book. She highlights in several telling examples that children build their perception of a story by negotiating between logic and imagination which challenges the notion of linear developmental patterns. The contradictions reflected in the children's book and film related behaviour, she says, happily coexist in the mind of the child, frequently surprising the adults. My story of Daniel's reaction to *The Snowman* is really something which is part of a much wider idea of the impassive child which critics tend to avoid when talking about story narrative. As Lowe says of her children's study, Rebecca declared at the age of two years and ten months, 'I am Tigger pretending to be Eeyore . . .' (Lowe 2007: 45); and Ralph at three years and one month, said, '[t]hat tortoise is looking sad because he wants to be a real tortoise. Don't cry tortoise, I will make you real with my magic thing . . .' (ibid.: 49) and the learning between the real and the represented real is part of a huge learning curve.

To some extent this important question, 'about how well pictures by themselves can depict events that we can recognise as stories' is contrary to a Kantian idea on representation. This quotation presents a little too much high Romanticism on the idea of the sublime but it does speak to the idea of the image:

> when we judge the sight of the ocean we must not do so on the basis of how we think it, enriched with all sorts of knowledge which we possess (but which is not contained in the direct intuition), e.g., as a vast realm of aquatic creatures, or as the great reservoir supplying the water for the vapours that impregnate the air with clouds for the benefit of the land, or again as an element that, while separating continents from one another, yet makes possible the greatest communication among them; for all such judgments will be teleological. Instead we must be able to view the ocean as poets do, merely in terms of what manifests itself to the eye – e.g., if we observe it while it is calm, as a clear mirror of water bounded only by the sky, or, if it is turbulent, as being like an abyss threatening to engulf everything – and yet find it sublime.
>
> (Kant 1997: 130)

What we are opening the child's thoughts up to is exploring the wider significance. Not just to see the surface but to inquire into the depth of image and imagine what is beyond. But this cannot come to them in Kant's idea of the language and narrative of a poet when they cannot yet articulate that which they already know. They are still trying to find the means of articulation and the teleological judgements are part of the developing process, surely?

In thinking what this idea of counterpoint connections means we can expand on the critical terminology a little because it does help to think about how the text and image can be thought of in the preparation stage of a story. Understanding this process of reading the words and images is crucial to the understanding and writing process. By common consensus there are four main ways of balancing the different word and image combinations. As Nikolajava and Scott suggest, these can be grouped into complementary, symmetry, enhancement, counterpoint and contradiction, although of course there will be inevitable leakage across them.

Complementary is where the words and images fill all of the spaces, each reinforcing the other so that they leave little for the child to imagine as an inactive observer. And this does not sit easy with the idea of 'exploring' I highlighted earlier. And this is not just for picture books but for picture-based culture, such as animation films. The trick is to try and have a three-way dialogue, one through pictures, one through the image and the other through the reader/viewer's interpretation. For example, if the words in the text were to say, 'In my garden we are growing the biggest, yummiest strawberry in the world,' an accompanying picture showing a strawberry the size of a house is a bit of a giveaway, when the actual revealing could take more time. I can envisage a journey pulling the story through the street until the strawberry can finally be revealed. A page-turning exercise in such a story is like peeling the fine gossamer skin of an onion until it slowly reveals its inner wonder; a bit like burlesque where the stripping is the art. And, indeed, it is hard to imagine this boy's 'climbing' being represented on a single page without some strong page-turning ideas:

> So the man spoke truth! The beanstalk grew up past Jack's window, so all he had to do was to open it and jump on to its branches . . . then Jack climbed, and he climbed and he climbed and he climbed and he climbed and he climbed and he climbed till at last he reached the sky . . .

This made me think of Italo Calvino's wonderful and curious novel *Invisible Cities*. The novel is essentially a conversation between Marco Polo and Kublai Khan and there is a breathtaking piece of descriptive writing which conjures up the most amazing imagery:

> The Great Khan tried to concentrate on the [chess] game: but now it was the game's reason that eluded him. The end of every game is a gain or a loss: but of what? . . . Kublai had arrived at the extreme operation: the definitive conquest, of which the empire's multiform treasures were only illusionary envelopes; it was reduced to a square of planed wood.
> Then Marco Polo spoke: 'Your chessboard, sire, is inlaid with two woods: ebony and maple. The square on which your enlightened gaze is fixed was cut from the ring of a trunk that grew in a year of drought: you see how the fibres are arranged? Here a barely hinted knot can be made out: a bud tried to burgeon on a premature spring day, but the night's frost forced it to desist.' . . .
> The quantity of things that could be read in a little piece of smooth and empty wood overwhelmed Kublai; Polo was already talking about ebony forests, about rafts laden with logs that come down the rivers, of docks, of women at the windows . . .
> (Calvino, trans. Weaver 1974: 131–2)

And we can see how Kant's notion of the sublime is completely at odds with this. It is not just a square on a chess board but much, much more in a quest for exactitude. Calvino himself commented on this, saying,

> From the moment I wrote that page it became clear to me that my search for exactitude was branching out in two directions: on the one side, the reduction of secondary events to abstract patterns according to which one can carry out operations and demonstrates theorems; and the other, the effort made by words to present the tangible aspect of things as precisely as possible.
> (Calvino, trans. Creagh 1996: 74)

And this says a great deal to me about the exactitude of image and text when thinking about picture book construction. We can see how the juxtapositions work to the benefit of the narrative and story being constructed. Also, we can see how this chimes with the Kantian idea of a narrative poetics, which I referred to above, where the sea is not just the sea but a 'vast realm of aquatic creatures'.

But where Calvino's 'exactitude' and Kant's 'sublime' ideas merge is in their engagement with the idea of the extended Homeric simile (circa 850 BC[1]) in which the image takes on infinite possibilities and form, from which we can see storytelling ideas that are not new but centuries old. But even if the writer and artist calls time on the extended narrative the story goes on. As Harold Rosen (1985) says, 'Sentences end with full stops. Stories do not!' [2]

Symmetry is the simplest form of all, where both the words and visual images come to say the same thing. For example, if the words said 'This is the little red house' and were accompanied by a picture of a little red house, what we have is a static narrative which is more like a cue card than a story text. If handled well it can be quite interesting (and see my comments on *We're Going on a Bear Hunt* (Rosen and Oxenbury 1989, below). But the pictures and words only serve to duplicate each other and it might be said that the image is actually just an adornment. But as with 'complementary' (above) the pictures can be quite complex and the words should let them speak for themselves and vice versa, of course. Take this picture (below) for example:[3]

It is a composition of my desk right now as I take a break from writing these words and is entitled *Writing the Monsters Book* – original, huh? Don't you think the picture would have been more interesting without that title? So you could ask: why is the computer screen sitting on top of two books, one of them being by Sigmund Freud? Who are the people in the screensaver picture? What are those books on the shelf? Does that one say Murakami on the spine? Does that mug with the pens have *Lady Chatterley's Lover* written on it? Is that little figurine on the right African? What's written in the spiral-bound notebooks on the shelf? What's that glass ball thing to the left of the screen? What's written in the notebook on the desk? And this is just a sample of the images that could be explored. Hopefully this gives some idea about what we should be thinking about when approaching the words and images as composition. Because if we take this image and extend all the thoughts that surround it, the images and ideas, the books, the philosophical musings, the words I have written and the Homeric simile of my work station while sitting here, the picture only actually snatches a temporal moment in my time: and the 'hear no evil' monkey sitting on the speaker to the left is saying, 'enough'.

Before I move on I really should say something about the working experience and indeed comment on something that has been written about these two ideas on pictures because at this stage it should be said that I disagree with those who write that all too often the problems in the 'complementary' and 'symmetrical' issues in picture books are created because they are not produced by single author/illustrators, such as Maurice Sendak, John Burningham, Anthony Browne and Sven Nordqvist (one of my own favourites). From a personal point of view, it seems too simple to say, 'too many double-author picture books produced in the United States [for example] are created by a writer producing a text that is then sent by the writer's literary agent to a publisher, which then finds a suitable illustrator . . .' It is an interesting point, but to add, 'The writer has no say in the choice of the illustrator or in the illustrator's choice of pictorial solutions . . . the final product is, in fact, not a picture book, but an illustrated book' (Nikolajava and Scott 2006: 16) is an odd conclusion. This is immensely reductive and the only way it can be a 'fact' is if the writers who wrote that take possession of the word 'picturebook' making theirs the only definition and because of this making any other use of it look like a (mis)-representation. And although I haven't used the singular word in their way I doubt the logic of their argument. The 'fact' is that this is not my experience in Europe or in the USA.

It is nonsense to say there cannot be successful collaboration in the picture-book process and of course Nikolajava and Scott do go on later to concede this point. But let me personalise it. I wrote a book called *Magic Mr Edison*; I never met the illustrator, Katja Bandlow, who lives in Berlin while I live in Brighton. But we co-operated with each other and with our editor Natascha Biebow[4] throughout the production of the story, where we often asked each other to accommodate changes in the words or the images for the benefit of the story. I also wrote animation films and worked with story boarders, illustrators, producers, directors, editors and so on in what was an extreme environment of co-operation. These were not illustrated stories in animation, they were collaborated films just like collaborative projects can become picture books – and I often find myself thinking of picture books as static films.

Think of it like this: if I write a script for a film it is part of the scriptwriting art form. If the script is then made into a film it becomes part of a different discourse which is involved in making a film. If I write a story of picture book length it is part of the literary art form that is writing; if an illustrator turns the story into a picture book narrative it is a picture book in the art form of picture books, just as a film of a book is a way of taking the narrative of the literature into another art form. But that does not mean close collaboration is not a consideration. As Martin Waddell has said, 'When I write a picture book text I am just at the beginning of a long process, in which the whole structure and meaning of the story will be re-interpreted by someone else, an artist who deals in images' (Waddell 1991: 26).

What I have found is that each person in the production process is working with an artistic sensibility. No one wishes the film or the book to fail because of their work. Everyone is pulling together for the sake of the piece of art being produced. And this is not so uncommon, indeed the popular *Charlie and Lola* picture-book maker of recent years in the UK, Lauren Childs, worked for Damian Hirst, collaborating on his 'dot' paintings. The simple way to think of this is that the art of each has as more to do with the artistic concept than who carries out the work. For me, the *Toy Story* trilogy (1995–2010) is a series of picture books in motion where the words and images complement each other perfectly. They are also a wonderful example of collaboration. I make this point here because the writer and illustrator, as separate bodies and separate from each other, need to understand the same ideas and ways to approach the production. Not all good writers are good illustrators and not all good illustrators are good writers but couple the right creative team and the effect can be quite astonishing because they combine to produce a narrative from different perspectives. Cianciolo says,

> The author and book illustrator are literary artists: authors tell their stories and create images with skilful and original use of words; book illustrators tell their part of the story and create images with skilful and original use of line and shapes, colour and shading. If one agrees that literature is an art, then one must consider that whatever image of reality or aspect of the human condition is depicted in a novel, picture book, poem or drama is an illusion of that reality. The image cannot be a mere mirroring of any aspect of life in it is truly a work of art. In a work of literary art the writer or book illustrator uses words or lines and shapes to create images that amount to a selective interpretation of the reality. The result of this selective interpretation is an illusion rather than a miniature reproduction of the reality that is depicted in or associated within the story. The illusionary image must be thoroughly identifiable and believable, yet it must not [need not] be exactly life like.
>
> (Cianciolo 1990: 25)

Let me now move on to the next balancing word and image combinations.

Enhancement is where the words and pictures provide alternative information to provide a stronger narrative. Obviously the level of enhancement can vary in degrees from being almost symmetrical and complementary to down right confusing but the idea is to get the child to be able to explore the images being provided while taking the thread of the story with them. Think about these words in relation to the picture and the message in the picture below them:

We have a bear hibernating at the bottom of our garden![5]

I see no bear, just a potential entrance to where it could be hiding or hibernating since it has been snowing and he 'might' live here in a story narrative. We can see how this suggestion works and how it can become the site of a potential starting point for a story line.

> 'There's a bear called Fred, in our garden shed.'
> 'Really and truly?'

The bear doesn't have to be there to be really real. Of a fragment of a story like this, Foucault might suggest, 'An art of language is born whose task is no longer to sing of the improbable, but to make what doesn't appear – what can't or mustn't appear – appear.' Because it has a 'double relation to truth and power' such a narrative, such an art of language, 'sets itself up in a decision of non-truth: it explicitly puts itself forward as artifice, but while undertaking to produce its effects of truth' (Foucault 1979: 90). One of my own favourite paintings which works around this idea is Pieter Bruegel's *Landscape with the Fall of Icarus, c.* 1558 in the Musées Royaux des Beaux-Arts de Belgique, Brussels.[6] Apart from the title of the painting, you would hardly know it was a picture about Icarus at all unless you looked really closely for a tiny pair of legs sticking out of the sea in the bottom right hand corner.

Indeed W. H. Auden describes it wonderfully in his poem *Musée des Beaux Arts* and as a 'textual intervention' on the picture it is an extension of that Calvino and Kantian idea I was talking about above, where the ordinary and extraordinary combine to create a much larger narrative of the cultural event, and the Homeric simile extends beyond the initial telling of the Icarus story, which I came to via Ovid (43 BC–*c*. AD 18) and marched across the centuries.

Counterpoint is when words and pictures offer the reader alternative information so that an effort must be made to explore the connections therein and there are many varieties of counterpoint which can be explored. I am paraphrasing them and making some minor adjustments but the acknowledgement is theirs, see Nikolajava and Scott (2006: 24–6). They refer to them as:

- *Counterpoint in address*, where textual and visual gaps are deliberately left to be filled differently by the child and adult.
- *Counterpoint in style*, where words can be ironic while pictures nonironic and vice versa.
- *Counterpoint in genre or modality*, for example combining words of realism with fantasy images, my own favourite being Anthony Browne's *Gorilla* (1983).
- *Counterpoint of juxtaposition*: the *Granpa* (1988) story I discussed earlier is a perfect example of this where we have the story of the granpa and granddaughter side-by-side.
- *Counterpoint in perspective*, or point of view: a distinction is made between who is speaking (in picture books expressed primarily by words) and who is seeing (expressed either metaphorically, by words, or literally, by picture).

- *Counterpoint of metafictive nature*, where words can express notions that cannot be portrayed in images, 'I love you' being the obvious one although it will take a child a while to get this:

I ♥ you! U make my ♥ ♪♪

- *Counterpoint in space and time* is about the spatiotemporal and the only area in which words and images can never coincide. The picture, the verbal text, is mimetic; it communicates by showing. The verbal text is diagetic; it communicates by telling. But this is not conclusively so. Is this a picture of a rabbit or a duck (or neither)?

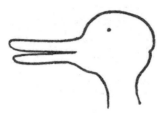

Wittgenstein puts it this way:

> Should I say: "The picture-rabbit and the picture-duck look just the same?"! Something militates against that – But can't I say: they look just the same, namely like this – and now I produce the ambiguous drawing. (The draft of water, the draft of a treaty.) But if I now wanted to offer reasons against this way of putting things – what would I have to say? That one sees the picture differently each time, if it is now a duck and now a rabbit – or, that what is the beak in the duck is the ears in the rabbit, etc?
>
> (Wittgenstein 1980: 16e)

Of course on the issue of 'draft [draught] of water . . . draft of a treaty', we can see how the verbal sound can confuse the meaning too. But this is no place to debate the Wittgenstein ideas on seeing.

- *Counterpoint in characterisation*, where words and images can present characters in a different and contradictory manner, thus creating irony and/or ambiguity and **contradiction** is the most extreme version of counterpoint which can have an immensely subtle effect, as I will now demonstrate.

She arose next morning and threw the curtains back. A ghostly white frost sparkled everywhere. Alice was the last person left on the island. So no one else could see how beautiful it all was . . .

I am not going to insult your intelligence by trying to translate this text and image combination for you but Jacques Derrida said, 'as always, coherence in contradiction expresses the force of desire'.[7] At best this is a clumsy contradiction but we can see how the combinations enhance the storyline. It is a bit like those *Scream* movies: Alice is alone – or is she? After all, who wrote the ghostly Merry Christmas message etched on the icy car window?[8] And when we are considering this we also need to consider Scott McCloud's

point in his immensely useful book *Understanding Comics*, where he advises that, 'the simpler the representation of the object, the further it is abstracted from reality, and so the greater the burden of interpretation upon the reader' (McCloud 1993: 46–8, cited in Hunt 2001: 288)

But writers and artists should not get too immersed in all of these ideas, all of the time. This is a critical intervention on a creative process. Creatively, it has to be a natural and spontaneous process, not clumsily constructed, and often when words and images are used together they interchange and alternate between several possibilities. These are just here to get you to think about the possibilities in the creation of the story. What is extremely important is you are telling a story to a child who is already exploring the language to understand and articulate their own story. But if we need any encouragement, now, to think of this is as 'mutual' exploration we need to consider what Andrew Cowan (2011) has recently written on this. He writes,

> I think the truest thing I can say about my own experience of writing is that I don't know what I am doing. Writing is the activity where I feel most adrift, least competent, most uncertain, least aware. I stumble along. And of course I'm not the only one.

> David Malouf: Writers have to be – naive is the wrong word – but in a state of innocence when writing. Everything you think you know you have to let fall out of your head, because the only thing that's going to be interesting in the book is what you don't yet know. Fixed ways of reacting are useless. Although you have to be highly conscious on one level – technique and so on – you also have to be in some 'non-knowing' mode for the book to shape itself. (Malouf 1996)

William Trevor: I believe in not quite knowing. A writer needs to be doubtful, questioning. I write out of curiosity and bewilderment. (Trevor 1990)

I rather like this image of a writer and a reader exploring the same experiential space in which both are questioning and trying to articulate meaning. Though importantly we can also say that the story they allude to, can identify a writer but in picture books there are actually five storytellers: one is the writer of the story, another is the illustrator, a third is the reader of the story, fourth is the central character who leads the story into what happens next and finally there is the child receiving it because he or she is not a 'passive' recipient but an 'active' explorer; which might also say that to some extent we are all stumbling along, trying to make sense of it all.

And this seems to be a good time to share Shirley Hughes's (Fearne 1985: 78) description of her methodology in creating a picture book, and I point you to the only italicised phrase in this quotation.

An illustrator's most intimate expression, the one closest to the heart, is in designing and writing a picture book. Ideas float about like icebergs, mostly below the surface, for a long time before you start putting pencil to paper. In my case they float by in pictures seen in my head. The simple sentences which appear on the page take as much time in the writing as a much longer piece. Onion-like, the finished text should be smooth and rounded, but inside its layers and layers of thought and lots of rigorous editing. Next comes the making of the dummy, deploying the words and pictures into a 32 page format. I cut up blocks of text and reposition them on the page, drawing around them rapidly with a pencil or a felt pen. The dummy finds itself in the hands of the publishers, who address themselves into the many considerations of printing, foreign rights and advance publicity. I then immerse myself for three or four months embarking on the finished artwork. I do the colour work to the same scale as it will appear in print, using a sepia underpainting which I then work up with chalk and gouache, finally bringing up the original drawing with a very fine brush. It is a meticulous process which can't be hurried. There is no excitement to compare with sitting down with a blank piece of paper on the drawing board. You can be fairly sure that the book you produce will – for young children – be a *shared experience* for them, and they will be looking at the pictures with a grown up or an older child, pointing things out to each other and extending one's visual range. If the child is reading the book, they can take the narrative at exactly the pace they want to, can turn back the pages, compare and imagine things for themselves. A good book will bring out from its audience as much as they care to give.

Crucial to all of this is an understanding that exploring writing for early years is more than just thinking about the words on the page. Ideas on literacy and understanding are dependent on many more factors than just being able to read the words and enjoying the shared experience. And, indeed, leaving a child who cannot read with a favourite book can only help them to begin making up their own version through mimesis or through sheer creative ideas.

If you have ever seen a child flicking through a well-loved picture book on their own, speaking (not reading) the memorised story and engaging with the book as an object of pleasure and familiarity, you will witness a different experience from the intimate triangular one referred to above beginning to unfold: it is one of engagement with the book and book as story and story as experience. Hazard said,

> a book that remains faithful to the very essence of art; that offers an intuitive and direct way of knowledge, a simple beauty capable of being perceived immediately, arousing in their souls a vibration which will endure all their lives. Enchanting pictures bring release and joy; books that enable children to share the great human emotions, give them respect for universal life; that teach them not to despise everything that is mysterious in creation or in men; books that distil from all the different kinds of knowledge the most difficult and most necessary – that of the human heart; books that have the integrity to perpetuate their own faith in truth and justice, that contain a profound morality without preaching or teaching, that set in action truths worthy of lasting forever.
>
> (1947: 43–8)

OK, it is a bit dated and optimistic but there is a charm to what he is saying, especially when we bear in mind that it was written at the end of two very brutal world wars and we can surely forgive his innocence to experience wordplay here.

Chapter 7

More monsters and bears

The aesthetic strength of a picture book is determined by its combination of words and images but much has to be noted in the wordplay. Picture books such as Michael Rosen's *We're Going on a Bear Hunt* (Rosen and Oxenbury 1989) continue to be popular with young children long after the first 'reading'. This is partly because while its visual composition conveys a good sense of motion, a journey there and back, what really pulls the story along, to paraphrase Margaret Meek, is the rhythmic sense of the wordplay. The fact that the book can be acted out, makes it more like a game than a reading exercise; it is a fun, interactive story of a family on a journey which lends itself to a textual event beyond the mere reading of the book. Built on the old 'bear hunt' campfire chant,

> We're going on a bear hunt.
> We're going to catch a big one.
> What a beautiful day!
> We're not scared.
> Oh–oh!
>> (Rosen 1989)[1]

The narrative is intelligently set up with the repetition of these five lines pulling the child into the action. But the symmetry of the book is equally important to the story, even though the symmetrical link between the words and images is fairly standard and indeed symmetrical, in the word and image balancing I mentioned above. What you see is what you get in a typical nursery rhyme manner. But the story is not static but has wonderful movement, not to mention the all important element of surprise. I know it says, 'we are going on a bear hunt,' but you don't actually expect to meet one – but when you do you have to run all the way back to the beginning again to hide! It is a great example of a voyage and return narrative[2] while one that incorporates overcoming the monster, and I can agree here that,

> the advantages of picture books are threefold: this mixed media has its own aesthetic value, it employs many sophisticated narrative techniques in immediately accessible ways, and it encourages children not only to discuss the stories but also to share and talk about the actual process of reading. No other literary genre gains the willing collaboration of its readers so readily.
>> (Ratcliffe, cited in Wallen (ed.), 1990: 15)

Of course, the bear idea is pictorially and verbally wonderful. I recall another from my children's childhood called, *The Bear Under the Stairs* by Helen Cooper (1994), a story to help children address fear of the dark. But just like the title for this book, *Monsters Under the Bed* it relies on a huge Coleridgeian suspension of disbelief that children have. There are no monsters under the bed just like there are no bears under the stairs but as a source of exploration in a children's story they are incredibly potent images. They are the imaginative shadows, the instantly recognisable forms; and as every writer, especially of fiction, recognises, writing depends on the 'shadows of imagination [and] that willing suspension of disbelief for the moment.'[3]

This is put into context when Tom Davis asks,

> What do children dream about? All sorts of things, but one odd thing. They have a tendency to dream, and play, about monsters. Wild animals. Fear of darkness. Falling from trees. Jungles. Fighting. Being eaten. And traditional children's stories reflect these dreams. Why? My children were brought up in Mosely, Birmingham (UK). No monsters, no jungles, no serious danger of being eaten by wild animals.
>
> (cited in Boulter 2007: 50)[4]

And nowhere is this exemplified more than in the incredible and influential book, *Where the Wild Things Are* (Sendak 1963). Monsters and bears and the like, imaginary and real looking, give the reader a sense of wonder in the narrative process. But more than this, the child in the book (and the child reader) is situated right at the cusp of Lacan's imaginary stage I mentioned earlier, where the narrative leans on the known but the unworded images reflect that which is not yet known and therefore alien and where the wild things are. But fear of the unknown is normal; as Freud says, it is both a recognition of pleasure (and/or pain) in the offing, and is a secret form of pleasure in itself. In fearing 'where the wild things are' we fear life but the pull to those 'secret forms of pleasure' exist still. After all, Freud also said, 'Life is impoverished . . . when the highest stake in the game of living, life itself, may not be risked.'[5]

Indeed, as Sendak himself said with his usual candour in an interview with Art Spiegelman (1993) for the *New Yorker*, 'Childhood is deep and rich . . . It's vast, mysterious, and profound . . .' And in defending the dark nature and brutal honesty of his work for children, he speaks honestly and frankly, saying, 'You can't protect kids; they know everything' (cited in Zornado 2001: 171). As Zornado reveals, Sendak is controversial in his ideas but they are worth taking on board because they do address the Freudian idea of risk.

> 'You have to approach [the child] with ferocious honesty,' Sendak stated in yet another interview while speaking about his work in children's theatre. In fact, in almost every interview Sendak has granted, he speaks of the child's need for 'ferocious honesty' in whatever the child is presented with, be it a picture book or an opera. He sees his own work as a direct challenge to the general trend in children's culture. 'Most things published for children,' Sendak argues, 'are strictly for their parents and strictly for grandma, because kids have no money.'
>
> (Zornado 2001: 175)

You can see how this idea chimes with what Jack Zipes has been saying for years on the whole idea of the culture for children industry and the cultural homogenisation of culture.[6]

The more we invest in children, the more we destroy their future. There is no way out of the paradox that we have created, unless we consider our investment. For twenty-five years I have been engaged in writing about children's literature and culture. I have always written with the hope that childhood might be redeemed, not innocent childhood, but a childhood rich in adventure and opportunities for self-*exploration* and self determination. Instead, I witness a growing regulation and standardization of children's lives that undermine the very sincere concern parents have for their young. It appears that my hope for greater freedom and creativity in children's lives will be disappointed. Yet I have not abandoned hope. I have become more sober about changing how we socialize children, even though the way do it is nothing short of barbaric [my italics].

(Zipes 2002: ix–x)

Zipes goes on to address this at great length but this harks right back to what I said earlier about opening up potential channels for exploration through art and culture; if you, as a potential cultural practitioner and artist, are not aware of this what hope is there? And yet, as Zornado declares, and I find this fascinating,

Sendak resists the sometimes squeamish adult audiences and writes for an audience of children that he perceives as intuitively aware of what goes on around them, including the lies, the half-truths, and the sugar-coatings that adults apply to the world in order to 'spare' children. Sendak has never spared his audience, and this is nowhere more obvious than in his opera *Hansel and Gretel*, which depicts the Witch's oven as crematorium, or his 1993 picture book, *We Are All in the Dumps with Jack and Guy*, that depicts a children's orphanage-as-concentration camp.

(Zornado 2001: 175)

There is a lot of information resting in this quotation. At the same time that Sendak, like Zipes, despairs at the commodity packaging available to children he also resists it in his own work. And it is fascinating to see him say that he perceives children to be 'intuitively aware' of what goes on around them. Zipes' fears are that the longer children spend around adults the more they are likely to become contaminated by the paradox of their 'investment'. So as writers we need to think about taking up the cudgels. And by now it should be clear that I think it is a storyteller's job is to talk about 'where the wild things are' but also to show through the story that 'the game of living, life itself' is a risk. Just like little Max, children need to be able to know when to say no!

I was thinking about this other day when I was watching a child at play and thinking back to my own son who as a young boy had a fantastic imagination (something he still exercises). At the point of play the story in his head, and in his actions, was not about a little boy corresponding to an adult's idea of what a little boy should be or indeed as a representative of little boyhood. He was the adult and I, as I got down on my knees beside him, I was just the giant in his otherwise complex, grown-up (and growing-up) world of disseminating stories. He was the grown up in charge of the game and his thoughts; I was just the giant because I was taller and older and grumpier. As Jean Baudrillard says,

A strategy of this kind is far from innocent. It is the strategy adopted by children. Whereas adults make children believe that they, the adults, are adults, children for their part *let* adults believe that they, the children, are children . . . They *are* children, but they do not believe it. They sail under the flag of childhood as under a flag of convenience . . . It is in this sense that the child is other to the adult . . .

(Baudrillard 1993: 192)

It was Maurice Blanchot who stated that 'the writer never knows if the work is done', in fact 'the work of art, the literary work – is neither finished nor unfinished: it is.' (Blanchot 1999: 402). And in some ways this speaks for a child in the Baudrillardian sense, if we switch it around a little we could say, the child is not 'other' to the adult in any context, as I have said previously, he or she 'just is'. In play, the child is secure in the knowledge that while he may be unable to articulate his monsters, he can deal with them in his own thoughts. It is the unknown he needs help to explore.

I have no plans to give an investigative reading of Freud's essay 'The Uncanny' here but there is an underpinning idea. The Freudian idea of the uncanny is that it does not derive its shock effect from something strangely unknown but on the contrary, from something strangely familiar which defeats our efforts to separate ourselves from it. The original German title for 'The Uncanny' essay is *Das Unheimlich*. *Heimlich* is the German word for homely, that which is knowable and secure, but *Unheimlich* does not come to mean un-homely but that which is known and repressed, such as fear and desire. Of course, as I have said above and in *Here Comes the Bogeyman*, Baudrillard is wrong to say 'the child is other to the adult . . .' as part of this idea. They truly are in a process of becoming, not being, the woman, the black person, the gay, etc. Those other demographic categories are pretty much stuck with their markers. But a child is an identity under erasure; the child only has a few years before he or she is camouflaged as 'one of us' and not other to us. Reynolds (2007: 100) has written, 'Growing up involves making choices and shaping an identity. As a general rule, choosing one path, whether this is educational, cultural or social, closes down options . . .' and so the exploration is very important indeed.

It is now time to cross the border from picture books to those early read to/reading texts that are less dependent on pictures. But before I do this there is something I would like to cover first.

Chapter 8

Know the reading child

It is all too easy to say that trying to assess the age of the child being targeted by a story should not be a factor in the creative process. There are those who will say a good writing, a good book, a story well told will always find its reader. This is a story I have heard often but I do not believe it. There are many reasons for this and the publishing industry, in unofficial cahoots with the education industry, owns most of them. But this issue is not to be confused with the 'No to Age Banding' campaign.[1] So let's consider both points together.

The 'No to Age Banding' issue arose because publishers began putting recommended reading ages on book covers. This is not such a huge problem for younger children but imagine, if you will, being teased in school for carrying a book that says 7+ on the cover when you are eleven years old. The simple fact is there should be no stigma attached to reading.

> NASEN (formerly the National Association for Special Educational Needs) mirrored these anxieties, stressing, amongst other concerns, that the self-esteem of reluctant readers will be reduced and vulnerable children could become even more exposed to bullying from their peers if they are perceived to be reading a 'babies book'.[2]

Children should be able to read up and down age ranges. As Philip Pullman says,

> I don't mind booksellers putting my books on a shelf marked 9–11; I don't mind reviewers saying about a book of mine that it would be suitable for ages 10 and over. Everyone is entitled to an opinion. But I mind very much when my own book says, with an air of final authority, that it is intended for children of 9 and upwards, and everyone else can leave it alone. It's not for them. Because, as I say, that is *not information*. It's not true. I did not intend the book for this age, and not that; for one class of reader, and not others. I wrote it for anyone who wants to read it, and I want as many readers as I can get, and I want to meet them honestly. And the effect of this little printed figure will be to put at risk the relationship between the author and the reader, by introducing a falsehood into it. For a book to claim 'This was written for children of 11+', when it simply wasn't, is to tell an untruth.[3]

But this brings us to the other issue I raised above, which is that there has to be a general awareness of the reader's expectations from a book. Philip Pullman knows this too, and indeed he doesn't call himself a writer for children on his website, where he writes,

> My only real claim to anyone's attention lies in my writing. I've published nearly twenty books, *mostly of the sort that are read by children*, though I'm happy to say that the natural audience for my work seems to be a mixed one – mixed in age, that is, though the more mixed in every other way as well, the better [my italics].[4]

But in fact he is well aware of who his reading public are and it is crucial to your child recipient of the book that you understand for whom you are writing. But think about it, it simply wouldn't do to write something like this, and then expect a child to understand it.

> Lacan proposes that human infants pass through a stage in which an external image of the body (reflected in a mirror) gives rise to the mental representation of 'self' and thereby 'other'. The infant identifies with the image, which serves as a *gestalt* of her or his emerging perceptions of selfhood . . .

It is nonsense to say we can simply provide words in a story context and just send them out there without thought of and for the potential readership. Of course it is to be hoped you can and will understand what I wrote above in time. We, as writers and critics, still seem to be clear about one thing: a common sense should prevail. As Fred Inglis has argued:

> it is simply ignorant not to admit that children's novelists have developed a set of conventions for their work. Such development is a natural extension of the elaborate and implicit system of rules, orthodoxies, improvisations, customs, forms and adjustments that characterise the way any adult tells stories or simply talks at length to children.
>
> (Inglis 1981: 101)

The reading age of children is an approximation between ages five to fifteen before they are plunged into the exam-ridden world of teenagehood. Only last year, at the age of fifteen my son began to study *Of Mice and Men* (John Steinbeck 1937) and *The Crucible* (Arthur Miller 1953) having just come away from the fantastic William Nicholson's *Wind On Fire* trilogy (2000–2003). But let's not be coy about this. Child-centred culture, books, films, etc., have an audience and where children are concerned it is aligned to age and experience and if we don't try to target certain groups, not dictating, as shown above, but being aware of different needs, then the real problem is for some there will be no books. Just to take the simple argument, if everyone followed this idea from Pullman, 'Do what you truly believe in, and do it with all your might' (op. cit.), without regard for the reader, then what of the boy (already a troubled reader, aged seven, say) who only likes football and spaceships and just can't find anything he likes to read that is suitable for his reading ability? There should be books for all and Pullman agrees so make sure you understand this – and I will address this in greater detail in Part II of this book when I address the subject of writing

In the meantime, and going back to Lacan with some help from Kristeva, lists of age ranges are only an approximation of childhood and experience, but think of it critically. I discussed this above but let's put a picture book style timeline on it:

- Around 0–6 months age: Juliet Kristeva (1998) called this the *chora* stage and we can pretty well discount it from everything we are doing. It is the earliest stage of development, dominated by the chaotic mix of feelings, needs and perceptions which are life drives. That's not to say they can't have access to what might be called books but they are really at a stage when the child has an incapacity to differentiate between his or herself and everything else.
- Around 4–8 months of age: Kristeva (1998) posits the child between the *chora* and the *mirror* stage, which is still pre-linguistic even if cognition is beginning to make sense. The child only has gestures and little language to articulate his or herself. All a book could do is begin to introduce colour leading through the *imaginary* stage of development as he or she approaches the mirror stage.
- Around 10–18 months of age: this is the 'mirror stage' according to Lacan (1953). The child can identify her or his own image and is beginning to negotiate his or her relationship with others, entering the language system which is concerned with lack and separation and, at the latter stages, children are really beginning to differentiate and beginning to distinguish characters that are 'like-me' and 'unlike-me' and is looking on to the *symbolic*.
- 19 months to 5 years of age: this is the beginning of the *symbolic* stage. It starts to bring the acquisition of a differential system of language, which forever after determines the child's perception of the world around her or himself. While still in the *imaginary* stage and right at the start of the *symbolic*, in conjunction with attending school and the like they are stretching beyond the familial into a wider world of thoughts, ideas and images. These are the proper picture-book years.

In book terms this is a rough chart with a lot of slippage – because we cannot classify everyone under a number and it is dependent on many other things like social skills and language skills right down to household income and poverty (which has a marked effect on child literacy).

- Ages 1–3   novelty books that squeak, squash and can be chewed, nursery rhymes picture books – up to and around 800 words;
- Age 2–5   nursery rhymes and picture books – up to and around 800 words, early readers/read to books – collected stories, roughly 1,000–1,200 words each, perhaps four stories in an edition, like a *Dilly the Dinosaur* collection;
- Age 4–7   picture books – up to 800 words early readers/read to books – collected stories, roughly 1,000–1,200 words each, perhaps four stories in an edition, like a *Dilly the Dinosaur* collection;
- Age 6–9   chapter books – around 2,500–5,000 words eventually rising to around 13,000, series fiction – around 6,000 words eventually rising to around 13,000.

None of the categories above are carved in stone, it's just an example, but take the time to research what is on the shelves: it's an easy thing to do. Also check publishers' websites, for example, Random House's website is split into age groups, 0–5, 5–7, 7–9 and so on (although the first one is a bit of a nonsense, see above and indeed how can anyone be aged '0'?). But check them out for more details because they are precise and concise while still containing a lot of information, for example *Magic Mr Edison*, is described thus:

When a tramcar frightens Dan's dog Charlie one evening, the chase leads them through a maze of busy Victorian New York streets to the house of Mr Thomas Edison. Dan is fascinated to discover the secrets of Mr Edison's light bulb, and dreams of a world where he'll have electric light at the pull of a simple switch. A dramatic story that recreates historical experiences and makes them memorable and relevant to the modern child's point of view.

So we have a clear view of what the book is about but also that it covers lots of 'key stage' literacy issues such as history (Victorian), geography (New York – or New Jersey to be precise) and science (Thomas Edison, invention of the electric light bulb etc.) as well as being a family, pet care and shaggy dog story, which Thomas Edison just manages to find himself in because actually all the geography, history and science is wrapped up in a story about a boy who loses his dog on the way home in the dark. The Random House catalogue for *Magic Mr Edison* tags it as: Early learning/early learning concepts • 5–7 year olds • 48 pages • Picture Book Format.[5]

And now we can think how this classification can be broken down even further. By thinking through the stages of child development we can tie them into the school system. And we can take the 3–7 age group highlighted by Nicholas Tucker (Tucker 1981: 46). In the UK, this age grouping manages to collect the following five school categories:

Age 3	pre-school
Age 3 to 4	nursery
Age 4 to 5	reception
Age 5 to 7	infants
Age 7 to 11	juniors

As can be seen from the publisher's details above *Magic Mr Edison* is for 'infants'. Although can I just correct something Jack Zipes hinted at indirectly? I didn't write it to make money, I wrote it to provide a story and to find a way of imparting the ideas that can be explored throughout the story.

But going back to the list above, clearly all of these children cannot fit into one picture-book and early-reader grouping so we need to consider how relevant this is. It is not just a case of writing a book and hoping for the best because if we break down their achievements to date, it is the period in a child's life when they will learn more than they will ever learn again. But if we break down the variances in experience it is quite huge. Quite clearly, a seven-year-old picture-book reader is very different from a three-year-old being read to, and just think what he or she has learned and explored in-between.

I will write on ideas of language later, in Part II, and this is not the place to enter the literacy wars being waged between the 'experimental psychologists' and the 'psycho-linguists', interesting though they are. But it does pay to be aware of developing language which the child is battling with on several fronts at once. As Saxton (2010: 4) writes, 'Language has different components, or levels, each of which must be tackled,' and I touched on this above, but he goes on to say the big four levels of language are,

Phonology:	concerned with the sounds of speech
Vocabulary:	the storehouse of meaning (words)

Morphology:	bits of meaning encoded in the grammar, like the plural ending – s in *dogs*
Syntax:	the rules dictating how words are put together in sentences

(Saxton 2010: 4)

And you can see how these all come into use in the picture book and early years reading text in relation to the ideas on images and representation which we looked at above. The whole nature of the language used in early years writing is policed by a need to say what is meant in the best and shortest way possible. This does not have to flatten the language, removing all sense of rhythm, rhyme and playful texture but it does require an awareness beyond what is needed when we write for adults. And as I go on to show in Part II, the secret here is to remember this mantra.

~~ write for children – not at them ~~

When Jacqueline Rose writes, 'childhood persists . . . as something we endlessly rework in our attempt to build an image of our own history . . .' (Rose 1994: 12) she is talking about us as adult writers in the process of writing and indeed our perception of our childhood past. But this is problematic, surely. The picture book child and the early reader is not living childhood as a history, their own or ours as refracted by the book, they live it in the present. Young children live and think in real time. Reflection, nostalgia and memory recall is a psychological development. We have to try and reach out to children as they live in this real time, but this does not mean trying to be them. This, surely, is the logic of the picture book. It is also why 'flashback' almost never works in the picture book medium – it is something a child this young does not comprehend. Of course, having written about *Granpa* earlier, I have to qualify this. Although while it does represent a granpa telling his granddaughter stories of his past, the story is told in the present and the reader/read to child reads it thus.

But don't just take my word for it. Next time you get the chance, ask a three-year-old child what they did, or what they got for their birthday, six months prior. You will see their sense of recall is a bit vague because the truth is they live in the present, and in real time. Even a game is happening in the moment. But in writing the picture book we must bring it to life and stimulate child imagination. Remember a picture book is for a child who is beginning to learn to visualise a future but is very much living minute to minute. So we simulate the projection of a future, not by regurgitating the past or the ever-same present, but by providing a promise of what life can offer to be explored. And I know I keep hammering this home but once again the book as a mediator in child development is not so much explaining or showing but helping the child to connect to what they already know from other parts of life and then allowing them to take the ideas forward into some-thing they may or may not have thought about but are ready to explore. The child will take the story you have offered and incorporate it with their own thinking to take possession of the knowledge the mutual exploration imparts. It is nurture in progress and the whole nature of culture, communication and media is ensnared in this web of tangled discourse that is the cult and culture of the child and childhood. I repeat Lacan's assertion:

> One can only think of language as a network, a net over the entirety of things, over the totality of the real. It inscribes on the plane of the real this other plane, which we here call the plane of the symbolic.

(cited in Belsey 2005: 4)

Chapter 9

Crossing the border

For a child, moving from *Room on the Broom* by Julia Donaldson and Axel Scheffler (2002) on to something like *Dilly Tells the Truth* (Bradman 1987) requires a huge leap of faith; faith in the knowledge that you are still coming to a story worth hearing. After all, from a purely aesthetic point of view we can see the cover of Bradman's book is nice and colourful but the pictures inside are different. Susan Hellard makes a great job of illustrating but these are line drawings, not colour plates. And the books are smaller with far more words on the page. But the difference is in the telling.

Picture books rely on pictures to enhance the story being told in very few words. Early reader/read to books rely on the text to give the information with a little help from an illustration. Remember a picture book is generally thirty-two pages long, with around twelve double spreads in which to tell the story. That means the scope for the image across double spreads and as single spreads is far greater than the early reader/read to format. In *Dilly Tells the Truth* there are four stories at around 1,200 words each over fifty pages. The first story in the book, *Dilly and the Medicine*, is told over fifteen pages, which hold only eight small pictures. So the entire narrative is pretty well word-driven, which is a big change from picture books. But it is also the moment at which the child moves into a more mature level of narrative discourse.

Taking the Dilly stories as an exemplary starting point, it takes the children of the story, Dilly and Dorla (the fact that they happen to be child dinosaurs is of no consequence – they are representational), through a series of domestic dramas. But the difference from *Granpa*, say, is that the dramas are delivered through text, pictures and dialogue. Here is a snippet which has a huge point to make on writing for children:

> The other day I was in my room reading my favourite book, *The Famous Five Dinosaurs*, when Mother came in to see me. She looked rather worried.
> 'Have you seen Dilly?' she said.
> Dilly's my little brother. Mother and Father and I all love Dilly – but sometimes he can be so naughty.
>
> (Bradman 1987: 1)

The first major point we can notice in this tiny quotation is the narrative voice and the point of view (POV). Because we are still at the border crossing let's go back to picture books a moment.

The fact is that the use of an autodiagetic, first person narrative doesn't really work in picture books. This has more to do with child development than anything else. And I agree with Nikolajeva and Scott on this issue when they say, 'While identification of the "I" of the verbal text in itself presents a problem for young children, the contradictory perspective of the visual text is rather confusing.'

> In a picture book, a first-person narrator would mean that, while we share his [her] point of view, we never see him [her] appear in any picture. For an unsophisticated reader, this would present considerable difficulties. But also generally speaking, the convention of visual communication, be it painting, film, or picture book, creates in us the expectation of seeing the protagonist in the picture, and this convention is valid even though the author has chosen to tell the story from the first-person perspective.
>
> (2006: 124–5)

This is not to say it cannot be done, but it is highly unusual. When you think about it, if you are reading a book to a child you are positioning yourself as the narrator, putting your voice into the book as the person inside the story while being outside it as the reader. And yet, as we move away from the picture book we see Tony Bradman launch straight into a first-person narrative in the Dilly stories by using Dorla as the first-person narrator. Dorothy Edwards uses this technique too in *My Naughty Little Sister* and then you start to see it all over the place, in Judy Blume's *Are You There God? It's Me, Margaret* (1970), Roald Dahl's *The Witches* (1983), Anne Fine's *Goggle-Eyes* (1990), and it is very important in the writing-for-children oeuvre.

But other things are happening in the short Dilly quotation. Although Dorla is a representation of the child being read to/reading, she herself says she is 'reading', and look at the intertextuality, she is reading her 'favourite book, *The Famous Five Dinosaurs*' (the intertextual clue is in the title, Blyton[1] fans) while still being able to confirm she has a mother, a father and brother called Dilly who can sometimes be very naughty and indeed that 'Mother' is worried about him. All of this information from a first-person POV in fifty-one words and we are immediately sucked into the story and the page-turning potential it offers.

But there is more to consider which I already have in *Here Comes the Bogeyman*; I apologise for again taking from that which you may have read before but it does highlight a different point. Taking the Dilly story as a representation, what the writer has done is to make 'connections between curiosity and nurture' and bring them into a normative situation (Phillips 1995: 2) through storytelling, where 'ideally childhood is a series of reciprocal accommodations (or 'attunements' as they are now often referred to in an uneasy mixing of analogies)' (Phillips 1995: 4). And it seems appropriate to say here (I am substituting 'analyst' in the original quotation for 'writer', why will be self evident):

> the [writer] is not only the one who is supposed to know; he is the one who knows that he is suppose to know, which is to know something of extraordinary consequence – to know, as every child does somewhere, the sense in which nobody knows the answers. Childhood innocence is not naive trust, it is incredulity (what the child has to repress is an ironic scepticism).
>
> (Phillips 1995: 2)

The (im)possibility of writing for children is preceded by the knowledge that children grow up by being listened to; but the adult writer does not have all the answers to child questions, all they can do is tell children stories about the connections. That is exactly what is happening in the Dilly stories, it is what is being rehearsed inside the narrative for a child to read, as I have already written:

> The idea of nurture is a persuasive one. The so-called space between the child and the adult/writer is actually the place where the two collide, where the story exists, where experience and knowledge is nurtured and where real contact is made. Children do catch their parents/storytellers up (it is what growing up is all about – it is why the process is nurtured) and so in the meantime, on their catch up journey the storyteller can only, '. . . tell children stories about the connections.' So the issue becomes not 'why should we?' write for children but 'how?': 'To say 'story' articulates our existence, our essence, our very being as a thinking species, is a fact but it is no longer enough. It is necessary to understand it.
>
> (Melrose and McCaw, in Butt (ed.) 2007: 24)

The 'full meaning of experience is not simply given in the reflexive immediacy of the lived moment but emerges from explicit retrospection where meaning is recovered and re-enacted . . .'[2] It requires awareness not only of the adult's own currency, 'words', but also of the cultural context and of the world that is being constructed through the story. But the adult recognises something in the child too, it is not a one-way-street of imposed power but a realisation that, wrapped up in the imaginative idea of a child and childhood, we adults do not have all the stories. Once again, in a few short words from Tony Bradman, we can see how Dorla is an inclusive part of the story with opinions that Mother can agree with and explore with her, as they both have to confront the naughty Dilly.

Fundamental to this idea is the revealing of Dorla as a child developing as a critic of story, representation and form while and at the same time a similar 'real' reading child is being confronted with it. Children learn what they like and do not like very early on in the story. They often return time and again to a well-worn book before moving on, and as Eve Bearne says,

> The sudden and proliferated range of texts and 'representations of the world' [that come to children] mean that it is even more critical for children to be able to exert discrimination and choice over the literacies and literacy practices which they encounter daily . . . it becomes imperative to be able to read and write with the eyes of a critic.
>
> (Bearne 1996: 318)

And this begins at a very early stage of children's development as the child tunes into the 'story' narratives provided in their lives. In the social interaction at home, at school, on the computer, on the television screen, and in books which play a major part in this development; we have reached the position that,

> in the twenty-first century the notion of literacy needs to be reconceived as a plurality of literacies and *being* literate must be seen as anachronistic. As emerging literacies continue to impact on the social construction of those multiple literacies, *becoming* literate is the more apposite description.
>
> (Unsworth 2001: 8)

But now it will be clear what we are engaged in here, in moving from the picture book to the early-reader stage, is that we are progressing the child into the grown up world of reading, writing, literacy and art as *affective*, as well as *cognitive* and *intellectual* thought, which is hugely important. The montage of such adult-produced cultural practices is not a passive pacifier for the curious child, but a site for exploration. But the exploration is twofold because it is both an exploration and an intimacy, as I have already shown:

> This involves several epistemological acknowledgements. One is to confirm that we are indeed dependent upon intimacy, and that it is incumbent upon us all to nurture such relationships. This is at the heart of the African philosophy of the self, *ubuntu*, the humanistic ideal that can be loosely translated as, 'a person is only a person in relation to others'. It is also at the heart of the communicative mode known as parrhesia: free speech, or openness; the speech that is about intimacy, honesty and truth. Intimacy is about communication with the other, and parrhesia is a form of intimacy that requires courage because there is risk involved in it: the risk of offending those to whom we are attached, the risk of hurting those we love, or those who love us, the risk of damaging our own reputation (Foucault 2001: 15–160).[3]
>
> (Melrose and Webb 2011)

What is necessarily set aside in early years children, it seems, is the idea that they have to set aside the fear of this risk. They come to the text through the security of trust and nurture and mistrust is a development they are yet to encounter, in most cases. Certainly there is a danger of betrayal and loss, but there is also elation, illumination, and emotional delight, and the raw vitality of being a person in relation to other people, to art and to ideas is beginning to take shape. 'Life,' wrote Freud, 'is impoverished, it loses interest, when the highest stake in the game of living, life itself, may not be risked'.[4] But this is a learned process and a sociological and psychological development which the 'early years' child will grow into, in time.

Part II

Chapter 10

Considering the monsters

Having spent Part I dealing with the critical aspects of the cult and culture of the early years child and childhood in relation to their access to art, culture and communication via words and images; and in summing up the critical problems, while addressing a way through to an understanding of what we should be addressing in culture for very young children, I now propose to concentrate on ideas of critical creative process.

Having such a long preamble in Part I was, I feel, very important. It is important to know what we are doing and for whom, so I make no excuses for taking so long in getting to this section. A broad understanding of the critical issues, discourse and key ideas is an important part in understanding and knowledge. There is an ongoing healthy, academic dialogue on this issue and engagement with it is surely desirable; I urge you to take it seriously. And indeed I do feel it was important that we explored and exploded some of the myths to try to understand what it is that writers and artists are doing, how we are engaged and what is expected of us as creative practitioners in a critical context. I often refer to this as a creatively critical and critically creative vigilance. There is much to consider for the cultural practitioner, of and for the child, and I have tried to make it as accessible as I can because the whole cult and culture of the child, children and childhood is a web of intricacies.

What will be extremely important to this section is the whole idea of *story*. Aristotle said the important thing in any story is the sequence of events and it is sequence which invariably takes us through the list of possibilities and plots. In early years storytelling the idea of sequential narrative is very important; they must be able to begin to understand that a story narrative is all about 'what happens next' in the page-turning process – not to mention the surprise and wonder of the story on each page, in picture and verbal form.

Nevertheless, those plots and possibilities, as Freud suggests, are not the mere invention of creative imagination; rather they are only a combination of components that are strange to one another. We only know what is coming next because of what went before, and even then a shadow, replete with contradictions, ellipses and silences, comes to fall between antecedent and intentionality to question the proposition that a story has unique meaning to be reproduced or translated in the first place. Cowan refers to this by taking a quotation from Currie in saying this problem of fictional knowledge brings him to what he calls, 'a rather busy intersection of contemporary thinking: it is Derrida's call of the Other, Badiou's unnameable, de Man's blindness, Lyotard's inexpressible, Beckett's ineffable, Freud's uncanny, Lacan's real, Conrad's secret and, for Wittgenstein, what lies beyond the limits of language' (Currie 2007: 124). And he addresses this by saying that it is a problem for the philosopher and critic to address but they can only do so after the fact of the narrative production. He goes on to say, 'since it is a problem that may only be encountered in relation to a finished work in the context of its consumption or reception in a discourse that doesn't allow for the work to be rewritten in response to that reception.' I agree this is the case, so few of us are able to re-write, re-paint and so on after the original work has been published or displayed and has then been critiqued. As he also goes on to add,

> From the perspective of Creative Writing, the problem comes earlier, and is some-what different, though it's a problem that might be approached in terms used by Mark Currie when he speaks of 'a combination of blindness and insight' and 'the interaction between . . . conscious projects and . . . accidental effects'. He doesn't mean this pejoratively. And, from a writer's perspective, it needn't be problematic since our attempts to write about what we know are so often undertaken in the hope that we might know more than we know we know, and that this knowledge will only become evident after the work has left us. The problem, always, is how to live with the uncertainty that this engenders, and how to resist reaching after the formulations and consolations of other discourses.
>
> (Cowan 2011)

And this idea that 'our attempts to write about what we know are so often undertaken in the hope that we might know more than we know we know, and that this knowledge will only become evident after the work has left us . . .' (ibid.) is an interesting and useful way of thinking about the way story works. But it is not the only view and it brings to mind something Richard Rorty has written (albeit controversially),

> You cannot . . . find inspirational value in a text at the same time that you are viewing it as the product of a mechanism of cultural production . . . If it is to have inspira-tional value, a work must be allowed to recontextualize much of what you previously thought you knew; it cannot, at least at first, be recontextualized by what you already believe.
>
> (Rorty 1998: 133–4)

Jameson responds to this by saying, 'On the contrary, it is a reinvention of the historical situation alone that allows us to grasp the text as a vibrant historical act, and not as a document in the archives' (Jameson, cited in Ross (ed.) 2009: 248). I have included this disagreement between Rorty and Jameson so as you can see there is a consistent ongoing disagreement on the issues relating to the transmission of story, and because I think it is important that we try to rationalise it in a critical and cultural context.

What is clear is that the borders between these ideas are extremely porous and hardly borders but lots of fragments ideas all rubbing up against each other with no empirical or definitive facts to cling on to. It is a set of ideas, forever interesting. In terms of storytelling though, I am persuaded by Walter Benjamin's idea that the words and images that make up the narrative are like the fragments of a vessel:

> in order to be articulated together [they] must follow one another in the smallest details although they need not be like one another. In the same way a translation, instead of making itself similar to the meaning of the original, it must lovingly and in

detail, form itself according to the manner of meaning of the original, to make them *both* recognisable as the broken fragments of the greater language, just as fragments are the broken parts of the vessel.

(cited in Bhabha 1990: 170)

As Paul de Man reveals, '[Benjamin] is not saying that the fragments constitute a totality, he said the fragments are fragments, and that they remain essentially fragmentary. They follow each other metonymically, and they never constitute a totality' (de Man 1986: 91).[1] Thus the story is collated fragment by fragment into a linear narrative. In 'On language as such and the language of man', Benjamin also wrote that, 'Translation passes through *continua* of transformation, not abstract ideas of identity and similarity': essentially that which is foreign to the original, if only the difference between storyteller's performance, cultural, racial or otherwise, erodes the original's structures of reference and discourse.[2] And these frames and structures of story are constantly being readjusted by children in their own exploration and a 'develop[ing] sense of assembling and reassembling the frames of their lives for themselves . . .' (Zipes 1997: 110).

As Zipes has also said, 'Storytellers cannot and should not pretend to be therapists, gurus or social workers' (1995: 223). All we can do is tell the stories and provide the books and films that help them to make the connections. And Italo Calvino's following caveat rings true, too, 'Literature is not school. Literature must presuppose a public that is more cultured, and *more cultured than the writer himself.* Whether or not such a public exists is unimportant' (Calvino 1982: 85). And now I hope you have spotted what I am doing here.

What we can see is a sample of the diverse words of thinkers such as Walter Benjamin, Richard Rorty, Fredric Jameson, Paul de Man, Jack Zipes and Italo Calvino tugging a thread of understanding through a pattern of discourse and thought that replicates Benjamin's fragments of a vessel. We never stop doing this kind of thing, of collecting the fragments and trying to assemble them into coherence, once we have learned how it works. And that learning takes place at a very early age, it is all about making the connections (now where have we heard that before?).

Remember, too, what I said about Nodelman's quote earlier. He suggests, 'a picture in a picture book confirms and makes more specific a story that is already implied by the context of previous and subsequent pictures' (1988: viii). And he is right. A random picture in a picture book stands in isolation. It can tell a story in its own right but the whole story relies on the preceding and following pictures for clarity and in maintaining the narrative thread. Even the movement from the front cover to the first story page has a context in this and I will reveal this in more detail below when I talk about the model for a thirty-two page picture book.

But, and this is really important to register, the writer and the artist doesn't have the luxury of the critic. Nor does he or she have the preceding picture for the story to follow, except as a fragment of their own experience. Indeed, T. S. Eliot opened 'Burnt Norton' in *Four Quartets* with such an idea when he wrote,

> Time present and past
> Are both perhaps present in time future
> And time future contained in time past

(Eliot 1944: 13)

As Jacques Derrida has written, the 'future, this beyond, is not another time, a day after history. It is *present* at the heart of experience. Present not as a total presence but as a *trace*' (1978: 95). And this could be rephrased as, the future story, this as yet unseen narrative, is not situated in another time, a day after history; it is present at the heart of experience; present not as a total presence but as a trace. And we can begin to see how these story connections work in context. As Jameson goes on to say,

> For now and today the participants [in this debate] are able to follow Deleuze's great principle that both art and philosophy think, only they think in different languages, the one with concepts, the other with its own specific materials. The philosopher produces new concepts, while the painter produces a new color, or if you prefer, a new brush-stroke, a layer of new oil paint. But the work of both is a work with categories, is a form of thinking and of experimentation with new thinking – a principle which obliges us to revise the very notion of comparison as such.
>
> (Jameson, cited in Ross (ed.) 2009)

So, when Cowan says 'our attempts to write about what we know are so often undertaken in the hope that we might know more than we know we know, and that this knowledge will only become evident after the work has left us . . .' (2011), it begins to ring true, for me at least. And I am reminded of T. S. Eliot again because he addresses this in 'East Coker' in the *Four Quartets* (1944: 26):

> So here I am in the middle way, having had twenty years –
> Twenty years largely wasted, the years of *l'entre deux guerres* –
> Trying to learn to use words, and every attempt
> Is a wholly new start, and a different kind of failure
> Because one has only learned to get the better of words
> For the thing one no longer has to say, or the way in which
> One is no longer disposed to say. And so each venture
> Is a new beginning, a raid on the inarticulate . . .
> For us, there is only the trying. The rest is not our business.

To repeat, it was Maurice Blanchot who said 'the writer never knows if the work is done' and 'the work of art the literary work – is neither finished nor unfinished: it is' (Blanchot 1999: 402), and all too often it is for others to discover the underlying truth or that might be meaning in the text. Like Don DeLillo, 'I write to find out what I know,' and then some more.

Thus, in thinking about child-centred discourse we have to make sure we know all that there is available to know. It is not just a case of 'we know what we know' but also striving to 'know what we know not' because in exploring the adult-provided, child-centred text the child, too, will be exploring what they know they know as well as that which they know not and have yet to learn and experience, which is always less than their adult counterparts who are engaged in the same discourse. And I hope this is clear because it happens to be very important.

I know these issues are complex and at times, gathered as they are like Benjaminian fragments, they may look deliberately opaque, but this cannot be helped: complex is complex, simple as. Crucial to all of this, however, is a very simple understanding. In a moment of understatement, the children's writer Chris Powling highlights a very important though obvious point when he says, 'Children see the world from the viewpoint of someone who hasn't lived very long . . .'; well, they are smaller, of course, so their viewpoint will be different. But it is something we have been looking at, not as a height issue but one of experience and we have to stretch Powling's metaphor from the literary to the more abstract idea. But he is right to add his own caveat that, 'none of us becomes so wise we can afford to dispense with sheer astonishment at existence and what it entails'.[3]

I would make more of a case than this. Dispensing with the astonishment simply reveals the paucity of the story of life itself, especially when writing for children. Culture for children, books, plays, films, art in picture books onwards should be about astonishment and surprise. But this is the case even for adults engaged in child-centred culture. Some of the work I have seen in my adopted home town is astonishingly good, like the festival called Burning the Clocks, which we could take it as an example; it is an immensely child-centred and child-friendly art in the community project, involving children and adults working together on making lanterns and thinking about the solstice story, followed by an amazing festival of artistic endeavour culminating in a spectacular bonfire. Burning the Clocks is intended as an antidote to the excesses of the consumerism, commodity fetishism and the commercialisation of Christmas. And it achieves this by bringing the community together in a temporal art spectacular which has an almost spiritual paradox. People gather to make paper and willow lanterns to carry through their city and burn on the beach on the shortest day, as a token for the end of the year. And as the pictures shows these lanterns can be very exotic indeed.[4]

As the website reveals, 'No lantern is better for its purpose than any other, all are unique to the maker and precious, but all are given up to be burnt to greet the lengthening days.' But such festivals go on all over the world. So the point is that while children are involved in such organised events, the opportunity to build on this through other cultural events is immense.

In witnessing the hugeness of such a cultural community event and the effect it can have on young children who are fully involved, actively not passively, in the making, marching and the burning with its underlying themes, which I have seen at first hand, we cannot go back to thinking that young children think simply and have little stories for their little minds. It is a mistake to think that just because they are smaller they are any less responsive to the new. Once again, and I keep repeating this, it is the combined intimacy, experience and connections that are being explored.

Indeed, their developing language too is a surprise when confronted. As I have written elsewhere,

> My son Daniel, aged four at the time, was sitting with a box of dinosaurs on the floor, naming them for me. This is an *Apatosaurus* and this is an *Iguanodon*. Invariably, as would often happen in these naming session, he would begin to construct a little narrative about them, such as this is a *Euplacephalus*, he bashes other dinosaurs with his tail (note the present tense). On this particular day, however, the story went like this:

'Now Dad, this is a *Tyrannosaurus Rex*, he's a carnivore because he eats meat. And this is a *Diplodocus*, he's a herbivore because he eats grass and leaves. But this one is really interesting, Dad. This is a *Gallimimus*, he's an omnivore. D'you know why? Because he eats meat and grass.'

'That *is* interesting,' I replied (proudly).

'But you know what's really interesting Dad?' asked Daniel.

'I don't know. Why don't you tell me,' I replied.

'We are omnivores. D'you know why? Because we eat meat and we eat salad.'

(Melrose 2001)

Daniel's story, told in his own inimitable and demonstrative fashion, which I have tried to retain, is both factual and precise. Think about how the story was constructed in a logical frame too, I for one found it interesting and insightful. But apart from revealing his ever-improving command of language, a command of multiple syllabic words and the delivery of fact in a story form, the deduction that we too were omnivores reveals the real magic of knowledge dissemination and his developing cognitive skills wrapped up in a story.

Of course, before long we were back on our hands and knees in his fantasy jungle where I was the giant in his world of play; where dinosaurs are real and the carnivores are trying to eat the herbivores, not to mention scaring the monsters that had somehow appeared from under the bed, but that was just as it should have been. Especially since this chapter is called 'considering the monsters'.

Although I can confirm that later on Daniel did ask me if I was 'Early Man' – well, what do you expect? Of course his early palaeontology was soon replaced by the popular culture of *Jurassic Park* (1993) directed by Steven Spielberg, but there is nothing wrong with that either. Access to story through popular culture is no less stimulating and, rather, it is part of the bigger picture in the make up of his own identity. I feel that sometimes and all too often, even today's critics can be a bit too precious about popular culture, especially when pontificating about 'story', 'storytelling' and what is good and bad.

The lessons a child learns in those formative years comes from the combination of child deduction and a healthy diet of the popular; the creative and the critical become part of his unconscious memory in building an identity and sense of self. When I was recollecting this story at breakfast this morning, his mother and sister (who was six at the time) could remember the 'Early Man' question because it stayed with me as a family joke for a while. But he couldn't remember making it, although he still knows what an omnivore is. The truth is this story could have been about many things, '*A Dog So Small* – a dog so small that you could only see it with your eyes shut . . .' to borrow from Philippa Pearce (Pearce, in Meek, Warlow and Barton 1977: 187); games of the imagination; flights of fantasy and cognitive development are all part of the same discourse. But why am I telling you this? Well, the answer is that it is a story.

Crucial to the following chapters will be the single word, story. This is the most crucial tool in the artist and writer's armoury. The narrative of a story exists implicitly in the experience it presents to be explored. It is the experience of temporal, human time, past, present, memory, the persistence of personal identity which is also an effect of the story narrative. This is because every story has a past, a present and a future. The story moves in time. At the same time that it allows us to comprehend its meaning it acknowledges the lived experience of time.[5] How else would story survive if it does not speak to us, other than as a trace of the past, with nothing to say in the present for the future? To repeat

Jacques Derrida's observation quoted above, the 'future, this beyond, is not another time, a day after history. It is *present* at the heart of experience. Present not as a total presence but as a *trace*' (1978: 95). But for me, time also filters through a continuing sense of historical justice despite the narrative of some of the doomsayers I have quoted earlier, because as I have also said, I am an optimist.

But this is all about making the connections, connecting the stories in making sense of the world that children occupy, so that they too can connect. I think it was Margaret Meek who once wrote that dealing with illiteracy in adults was difficult because they didn't understand how 'story' worked. And I am persuaded by this idea of Meek's, because it shows how important it is to address literacy at a very early age. As Meek also says,

> although it is possible to judge books for children by what are called 'adult standards' and regard them as part of literature, the young reader carries a different world in his [her] head, no less complex than an adult's but differently organized. He [she] needs his [her] stories in a different way, his [her] experiences of reading must be different. When discussing stories for children, to lose sight of the reader is too dangerous to contemplate.
>
> (Meek, Warlow and Barton 1977: 11)

This is an idea I endorse fully, and indeed have written about at great length in *Here Comes the Bogeyman: Exploring Contemporary Issues in Writing for Children* (2011) where I wrote,

> Going back to Nodelman's opening idea on the simplicity of texts, the problem lies in thinking how 'simplicity' in relation to texts can be defined, if at all, and indeed in using such terms may the text not also conceal the 'hidden child', lurking in a similar if not the same shadow? It seems to me that in investing a great deal of time looking for the (so called) hidden adult issues in child-centred texts then surely too the child reader may be reading something I as an adult may not? Because the question remains, while my fantasies and socio-cultural experience may be more inclined to reflect my ageing years they do not and cannot pretend to be the same as those of someone much younger although they are equally relevant to them. We should look at this more closely because Nodelman is talking about 'not childlike' being 'inextricably tied up in binary habits of thinking' (op. cit.) which, as I have already revealed, make me uneasy because I think there is both a 'hidden' child and adult in the text which is negotiated through the text and recognition of this is crucial.
>
> (Melrose 2011: 34)

Actually, in thinking about this, and in conjunction with the Lacan and Kristeva ideas I explored above in trying to help us frame the critical background, I thought of something else which may help to explain this thinking around childhood in early years. Although this may not be the best place to rehearse this debate, and I will not do so at great length, I was thinking that as young children move into the school system we can begin to detect what August and Friedrich Schlegel named the Apollonian/Dionysian opposition; a concept which was expanded and developed by Friedrich Nietzsche, who explains the two sides of the opposition as 'tendencies'. I am not here trying to laminate the present and stories of the ancient worlds, but it is not a new concept. Freud used

Oedipus, for example, and it is useful to see how elements of classical stories help to frame and display other ideas that occur. It says much for the power and longevity of 'story' too, so it is, I think, worthwhile pursuing.

The basic idea is this: the structure and rules of schooling follow the Apollonian tendency which is about order, clarity, and a controlling gaze, which manifests as 'peaceful stillness' and 'cognitive form' (Nietzsche 1993: 16). The Dionysian tendency is about play and adventure, risk and surprise, and manifests as 'blissful ecstasy', as 'a paroxysm of intoxication' (Nietzsche 1993: 17–18) and the playing while learning child falls into this storm of paradoxes when he or she begins to leave the imaginary for the symbolic and the real as they enter a learning while playing classroom. Oh my goodness, from *Dilly the Dinosaur* through T. S. Eliot, the solstice carnival Burning the Clocks and omnivores to Friedrich Nietzsche and the Apollonian/Dionysian tendencies,[6] I really must get out more. But as I have demonstrated throughout, it is all about making the connections: which leads us on to the idea of surprise!

Chapter 11

Surprise

I have used the word 'surprise' often and it almost seems too simple to be true, but one of the most crucial elements in writing for early years is the element of surprise. Young children come across surprises daily; it is part of their developing experience, both lived in and vicariously. As I have already written in Part I, Goswami (2008: 1–2, cited in Livingstone 2009: 16–17) writes,

> It is now recognized that children think and reason in the *same* ways as adults from early childhood. Children are less efficient reasoners than adults because they are more easily misled in their logic by interfering variables such as contextual variables, and because they are worse at inhibiting information . . . The major developmental change during the primary years is the development of self-regulatory skills . . . Cognitive development is experience-dependent, and older children have had more experiences than younger children . . .

and picture books and early years writing come in right at the beginning of this process as exemplary providors of both actual and vicarious experience. Children are not passive observers, they are constantly looking to experience the new. Thus the element of the new and surprising is intrinsic to the plural literacies that they are compelled to absorb daily. All of us are continually in search of this, are we not? We search for it in books and films and songs and poems: why else would we read and listen and absorb culture if it was just to address the bland and boring? What a dull world it would be if we became too grown up to be surprised by the unexpected.

But children are insiders in this process, not outsiders and one of the central assumptions underpinning *their* experience is the significant overlap between non-fictional and fictionalised patterns of representation, precisely because these symbolic frameworks or discourses are in circulation through popular culture as well as in real life situations, which a fictionalised and non-fictional, experiential narrative combines to inform. Remember what Webb said, above,

> there is little actual difference between the experience of physical stimuli, and the mental abstraction of reading and thought. This might seem unlikely; but . . . the gap between the 'real world' and 'mere representation' is not always as evident as common-sense would suggest. New research into how the brain works is shifting our understanding of how individuals make sense of the world, and convey sense to others . . . representation is considerably more that a simple matter of standing in for;

it is also productive of what we know, and how we know it: that is to say, it is communicative – it makes us.

(Webb 2009: 5)

As they grow through their childhood, children frequently draw upon references to and images from fiction, film and television drama and the internet in combination with their real living experience in constructing *their* stories. This has to be borne in mind when writing with child-centred thoughts and ideas. But surely the greatest element in any form of representation is surprise; it is what makes a good story great, good art great, good films great and I would be surprised if you were surprised to hear that.

Story narratives are what makes us human and they are crucial in the development of a child. There can't be any doubt about that. Storytelling is the way we convey the narrative of the events of our lives, dreams, memories, disappointments, fantasies, hopes, desires, fears, the list is endless. It is also the narrative of experience, the in-between place of cultural translation and the meeting place of engagement between the writer and the reader, the adult and the child. But the way stories are transmitted are many and multiple and multifarious, from the evening news to an encounter on a street corner; from a telephone call to a line from a poem stumbled upon on a tattered fragment of parchment or an internet website that drifted out of the ether and landed in your machine. And sometimes you can come across a story that is made for you, unbeknown to you, but is about you, even as a trace and yet even though you are part of the story the surprise is no less of a revelation.

For example, the first time I heard John Lennon's album *Imagine*, I was sitting on the dock of the bay[1] in Oban in the West of Scotland. It was in 1971 and I can remember it vividly. I was sixteen and instead of studying for my 'O' level exams I had been hitch-hiking around Scotland, trying to visit as many folk clubs and grabbing as many floor spots as I could during the Easter break from school. As I sat by the dock, just taking in the sunshine, the songs from the *Imagine* album were wafting out of a little yacht moored nearby.

Anyway, the owner of the yacht saw me and shouted over. He said he was taking a trip to the west coast island of Iona, did I want to come with him? Well, can you imagine? And to cut a long story short, later that day, with the tape still playing on an eight track loop (remember them?), we were sailing past the Isle of Mull toward the Sound of Iona when suddenly I saw something so unbelievably incredible. Out of nowhere this huge whale rose to the surface alongside us and spouted water high into the air. This is all very interesting, you might say, but why am I telling you this?

Well, because I was sixteen and feeling all adult and responsible for myself and then suddenly I realised what it was to be a child. There I had been all grown up and sitting on a boat with a stranger, listening to John Lennon and having a good time, and then there we were, two small people in a small boat, sailing on a big sea, confronted by a huge whale and I realised then that everything in the world was bigger than me and what a wonder it was. As our gaze followed the image of the whale, which was soon joined by others, our immediate reaction was one of *Dialektik im Stillstand* – dialectics at a standstill[2] (to paraphrase Walter Benjamin) – because that is the impact of such an event. That was the element of surprise which a developing child must encounter daily in the early years.

The moment became encapsulated in images that formed an arrested illustration of experience; an experience of something new which will not stand still, for it will never be new again, but will always be starting over as repeated images, in what Tiedemann called a historical constellation. Time was no longer past time, but, rather, coagulated in the imagistic configuration of the now; in the immediacy of the actual event as it unfolded. Can you imagine? Looking back now I realise that is what being a child is and I was lucky to be able to recognise it. At the point of surprise and disbelief we stop to gaze before we can react, it is the briefest point of intervention and intercession that comes before description; before language, which comes after with the realisation and then becomes the story and the story of the story and stories for they are all textual interventions, thereafter.

This story didn't even need these words to survive because the story is with me always. Stories go on and on and in a moment of nostalgia, long after the event itself I wrote this poem to celebrate and capture that memory, in the dialect I remember from that time.

> *Mind yersel' Jonah*
> It wisnae a trawler
>   wi' a net an' a hold
>   fuo o' fish dryin' in salt
>
> Nor Para Handy's puffer
>   puggie fou o'
>   Isla's best malt
>
> It wisnae a twisted wreck
>   wi' a hole in its deck
>   unco fou o' bones an' brine
>
> Nor an auld clipper
>   carrying tea fae the east
>   wi spices an' silks sae fine
>
> Naw this wis somethin' ither
>   somethin' mair muckle a' the gither
>   nowt a mere man wid sail
>
> And ah said, 'Mind yersel' Jonah
>   for she'll swallie ye hale
>   yon bloody great whale . . .'[3]

But then look how it links to a much older and indeed complete short story in the story of *Jonah* – which has to be one of the earliest short stories ever written. And yet at every twist and turn of the Jonah story surely he too is surprised in a childlike manner. Suddenly to be commanded to 'Arise, and go to Nineveh, that great city, and cry against it; for their wickedness is come up before me.' What combining these two pieces discloses is that art reveals time as temporal and as a site of historical method. What links the story I have just told between my personal story of the whale and the story of Jonah is intimacy, astonishment and the making of connections that can be traced back through centuries of storytelling yet still resonate together. As Althusser suggested,

> It is not enough, therefore, to say, as modern historians do, that *there are* different periodizations for different times, that each time has its own rhythms, some short,

some long; we must also think these differences in rhythm and punctuation in their foundation, in the type of articulation, displacement, and torsion which harmonizes these different times with one another. To go even further, I should say that we cannot restrict ourselves to reflecting the existence of the *visible* and measureable times in this way; we must, of absolute necessity, pose the question of the mode of existence of *invisible* times, of the invisible rhythms and punctuations concealed beneath the surface of each visible time.

(Althusser and Balibar 1997: 100–1)

The intimacy, astonishment and connections chime the visible and invisible rhythms and punctuations of the story narrative that is life, in making the connections: it all seems so simple.

As I said above, the Jonah story is one of the first ever known short stories. It has a classic, beginning, middle and an ending in storytelling parlance and this is what we are going to look at in the next section on story structure. But let us not forget the intimacy, astonishment and connections; the visible and invisible rhythms and punctuations of the story that reside therein and come to meet us across the ages because in the practice of cultural production that is what we are engaged in.

Chapter 12

Story and *Kyoto*

What I propose to do now is give you a rough version of a story I have written. It's not groundbreaking or particularly good for children in this state but what I aim to show how a draft of around a thousand words in a childlike story can be reduced to picture book length or extended to early-reader length as a means of demonstrating some of the issues I have been discussing. I have also written it in such a way that allows for the pictures to work at odds with the text to produce a bigger story than the thousands words them-selves. But when I explain the picture ideas you will see it as a little darker than it appears. This is just the bones of the story, the basic structure, but it is an attempt to combine a big story about a boy and a little bear – and a little story about global warming. And I know this might seem an unlikely combination but we have to think of the possibilities. What I plan to do is give the story straight and then play around with it, looking at different angles and ideas, both visual and verbal but just so you know, I am also going to tie it into my sailing to Iona, Jonah story too.

Kyoto

In the coldest country on top of the world, the boy was very happy. It had been a long, dark winter. But today the sun was shining. He waved goodbye to his mother. Then he yelled, 'Wee . . . ee . . .!' as he dived onto his sledge.

Nearby, a little polar bear looked happy too. She had been hibernating all winter with her mother. But now it was spring. Her mother nudged her gently into the snow. Soon the little bear was off exploring.

The yellow sun shone brightly above them.

The boy pulled his sledge up the side of a big snow hill.

The little bear climbed up the other side.

At the top of the hill they both had a brilliant view. The land was like a white desert, covered in snow. The bright yellow sun sent ripples of pink and orange and red colours shimmering across the ice.

Then the boy pushed his sledge down the hill and jumped on board.

Once again he shouted, 'Wee . . . eee . . .!' as he slid down the hill.

The little bear slipped down onto her bottom. She too began to slide down the hill. She didn't say anything (because bears can't talk).

Down and down and down they slid, slipping and sliding.
The boy couldn't see the little bear.
And the little bear couldn't see the boy.

Suddenly there was an almighty crash.

The boy and the little bear had bumped into each other at the bottom of the hill.
'Oi!' said the boy. And he laughed.
The little bear didn't say anything (because bears can't talk). She just jumped up and shook snow all over the boy.
'Oi!' laughed the boy again.

Then something very strange happened. The ground beneath them began to move.
It felt very odd indeed.

The boy and the little bear wobbled from side to side.
They had landed on ice.
The ice trembled and cracked.

Then it broke away and began to float out to sea.

At first the waves were gentle.
The ice only bobbled a little.
But suddenly the waves grew bigger and bigger, taking them further and further out to sea.

Up in the clear blue sky, the sun seemed to shine brighter than ever.
But the boy and the little bear began to feel very dark inside. So they moved closer together to become friends.

Soon the two friends couldn't see any more land.
They passed by a huge iceberg. An enormous whale surfaced to take a look. Then it disappeared again. The boy and the little bear were alone. Floating on the big sea they felt very small indeed.

'I'm cold,' said the boy.

The little bear didn't say anything (because bears can't talk). But she had her thick fur coat to keep her warm. So she huddled up to the boy to keep him warm too.

After a very long time at sea, the two friends felt the ice wobble again.
Then it landed with a bump on a seashore.

Both the boy and the little bear jumped onto the beach. Everything looked dirty and strange! Not clean and white like their home. But the worst thing was the noise.
All around they could hear the clanking and clanging and banging of factory machines. They huddled together again.

Suddenly the little bear heard a loud, scary noise roaring behind her. The boy pulled her back just in time. A huge coal lorry thundered past them. Then another and another!
'Phew!' said the boy to the little bear. He had never seen such monster lorries before.

Then more lorries sped towards them.
The boy and the little bear tried to run away . . .

. . . but they were too late.

A huge digger scooped them up with the coal and dumped them right on top of the coal mountain. Then the digger dumped more coal beside them. Then it did it again and again . . .

The monster lorries and dumping diggers and smoking chimneys and the noisy factory machines rattled and clanged. The noise frightened them.

Suddenly the boy laughed at the little bear. She was covered in coal dust.
'You look more like a panda than a polar bear,' the boy said.
The little bear didn't say anything (because bears can't talk).

The little bear looked very sad. So he wiped the dirt of her face with his sleeve. And they both stared out to sea.

Suddenly, the boy had an idea. He pointed to a large wood plank. It looked just like his sledge back home. It was nearly buried under a pile of coal but the two friends pulled it out together.

They climbed onto the sledge. Then together they began sliding away from the dirty digger, towards the sea.
Down and down they sledged . . . until they landed with a squelch.
But it was so muddy at the bottom they couldn't stop sledging.
They kept slithering and sliding across the ground . . .

. . . then they slid back onto the sea again, just like before.
And every wave took them further and further away from land.
The noise and the lights and the smoky dirty town disappeared.

Once again the boy and the little bear snuggled together to keep warm.
Once again they were alone on a big sea and they felt very small indeed.

After being out to sea for a long time, the little bear looked at the horizon.
Then she suddenly jumped into the sea.
'Oi!' said the boy, he didn't want to be left alone.

But the boy wasn't left alone.
Bears are very good swimmers and the little bear was pushing the sledge.
It soon landed with a bump on the seashore.

This land looked familiar. Everything looked normal.
The boy and the little bear jumped onto the ice.
The boy's mother waved at him.
The little bear's mother roared.

'Where have you been?' asked the boy's mother.
The boy looked over at his friend.
'Looking after the little bear . . .' replied the boy.
The little bear looked back at the boy,
'. . . and she was looking after me!'
The little bear didn't say anything (because bears can't talk).

★★★

OK, it can't be judged on any merits (or demerits) as it stands; it is just a story that I can use to demonstrate what I want us to address. At around one thousand words it can be pared down as a picture book narrative when supported by pictures or beefed up as an early reader to let the words paint the picture. As I said, it will allow me to highlight some important issues. The most important of all is the idea that, 'Any work of art must first tell a story'. This quotation is attributed to Robert Frost, and as I have already indicated,

> In reading this book, you have already decided to write for children and you are looking for guidance. You already think you have a story and you want to learn how to tell it well. Your reasons are immaterial. You will already have some idea of what kind of story you want to write. Whether its mystery, thriller, fantasy, science fiction, historical or whatever, the story will be germinating inside of you. But one thing is for certain – it will always be a *story*.
>
> (Melrose 2002: 16–17)

The first thing we should consider is the structure of the story as it stands, but before we do let me just give some back ground, visual ideas to help put the story into context.

Kyoto – visual ideas

The first thing to note is that at all times the vastness of the world is brought into context (and stark contrast) by the smallness (and innocence) of the boy and the little bear, but it is intended that the scenes can be visualised as moving freely, scene by scene, like an animated film . . .

Arctic home

A snowy landscape in bright spring sunshine, the boy and the bear are outside after a long dark winter so it's a scene of joy.

The boy and the little bear climb a snow hill (big for them because they are little) – the landscape is one of great ice-clad beauty.

The boy slides down the hillside on his sledge, the little bear slides down on her bum.

The sliding continues – until they crash at the bottom – possibly composite picture – but once again it's a picture of fun and joy, even when they crash together at the bottom.

Then strangeness enters as they land on the ice and it begins to break away and float out to sea.

All at sea

The big sea and the boy and the little bear (floating on the ice) begin to show the contrast of their size compared to the vastness – they also become friends.

The iceberg and the whale (in their vastness) dwarfs them as the boy and the bear huddle together for shared comfort – as friends do.

Land ahoy

The clean snowy landscape gave way to the sea, now the sea gives way to an industrial landscape – dirty and strange, smoky and noisy.

Dirty old town

Monster lorries and coal mines and factories, our innocents are abroad. The boy saves the bear.

Coal mountain

A monster digger scoops them up and dumps them on top of a coal pile (looks like a mountain to them). The little bear looks like a panda because of the coal dust. From the top of the pile they can see the landscape in all its dirty, smoky, noisy glory (it's hell).

Then the boy spots a makeshift sledge and they have to pull it out together. On a composite slide down the other side of the mountain – fun and joy. At the bottom they hit some mud etc. and keep slipping and sliding . . . and the fun and joy disappears . . ..

All at sea – again

Finally they slide straight into the sea again, the water splashes the coal off the little bear – the dirty town fades and they become very small on the sea again.

Arctic home

The homecoming – the little bear leaves the boy on the raft/sledge – then she pushes it to land. The reunion can be seen since the two mother's are waiting, they are back where they started, back to the clean, snowy landscape and a reunion where the premise to the story is revealed because this is going on behind them. 'Kyoto' is not the name of the little bear but an idea – no words necessary.

© Andrew Melrose, 2011.

Chapter 13

Story structure and characters

Assuming you do have something to say then, in its most basic form, a story can be broken down into six very basic elements: Balance, Disharmony, Inciting Incident, Problem, Resolution and Consequence or Resolution. Let me open this up by giving a simplified example from *Kyoto*:

Balance

Yesterday all was calm, spring was beginning to push away the long winter but nothing much was happening except it was getting warm. I didn't write this scene; other than reporting the domestics of the boy and the bear getting ready to greet the day, what would have been the point?

Disharmony

The boy and the bear are exploring their own side of the hill, the boy sledging and the little bear falling in the snow, which she had never seen in this state. They bump into each other at the bottom of the hill and are not quite sure what to make of each other – they are, after all, natural enemies.

Inciting incident

Just as they are coming to terms with each other the ice flow they are standing on begins to crack and break up and then suddenly they are on their own personal iceberg and floating out to sea.

Problem

They are both too young and small to know what they are going to do and so they are reluctant adventurers on a big sea. But things will get worse before they get better. They land on an industrial beach, are confronted by monster machines and noise and the clamour of an industrial wasteland. Even worse, they are scooped up onto the coal mountain.

Resolution

The boy sees a wooden plank or a pallet and tugs it out so they can slide down the mountain; he helps the bear. Whereupon they slip into the sea and do the return journey back to safety and home; and the bear helps the boy.

Conclusion

> Look after your friends and they will look after you, but the message is confused by the oil rig looming in the distance, so the wider narrative is if we don't look after our world it will not look after us – hence, Kyoto!

Clearly, the simplicity of the story allows huge licence for the illustrator who can capture the vastness and the hugeness of the images, the big journey for little people and back with a big message on friendship and a little message on global warming. The extended domesticity of the story allows the illustrator licence to play with the contradictory visuals. As Freud wrote, 'the storyteller has a peculiar power over us; by means of the moods he can put us in to, he is able to guide the current of our emotions, to dam it up in one direction and to make it flow in another (Freud 1990: 339–76), and this story is intended to have this kind of impact.

So it is a simple structure for a simple story but what has to be remembered is that written simply like this, without need to pause on literariness, literary dexterity and spending time on the visual narrative, it does not preclude the potential for sharing and exploration of the issues the story presents – or indeed, the need to know what happened next which was the secret to the story's success. And crucial to all of this is 'conflict' and 'cause and effect'. Freud refers to this conflict provision in his essay, 'The Uncanny' (Freud 1990: 335–76) when he also translates the German word *Unheimlich* into something stranger. The *Unheimlich* (literally the unhomely) is not the opposite of homely but that which is hidden and repressed. We accept and cope with everyday events and conventions as homely but we repress the *Unheimlich*, unhomely potential problems. Yet it is the *Unheimlich* that promotes change in a story. It is the monster under the bed. The two children in the *Kyoto* story (because the bear is surely a child in representation too) are in a homely situation without knowing the *Unheimlich* is lurking, and to use the old pantomime phrase, 'he's behind you'! As Freud says,

> The uncanny as it is depicted in *literature* . . . is a much more fertile province than the uncanny in real life, for it contains the whole of the latter and something more besides, something that cannot be found in real life.
>
> (Freud 1990: 372)

Crucial to this, however, is the knowledge that this very basic story template is just that, basic. But knowing this is very important. You can play around with it a little after you have mastered it as a basic model.

I have seen a great deal of samples of writing from apprentice writers who want to write but just don't know how to sustain the storytelling in a tight and coherent narrative structure. Just take the story above, for example, what would be the point in the little bear getting tangled up in some Japanese bindweed and taunted by some stroppy starlings in the industrial scene if none of these things added to the story? In fact it merely becomes a distraction because the task is to get back as soon as possible.

Of course, playing around with the basic form is a writer's privilege but knowing the basic rules helps us to understand the process much more easily. As I have said previously, Picasso was an accomplished fine art drawer before he began to break the rules of form and structure in his art. Storytellers are no different: there is an art and craft to writing and representation, and knowing this is really important to any writer. Know the rules before you break them, it's a simple idea.

Traditionally, then, this simple story would be set out as follows as I revealed before (Melrose 2002) and also when I was talking about the Jonah and *Kyoto* story:

Beginning

Meet the main character(s) and introduce the problem.

Middle

Focus on the problem, which gets worse through the inciting incident – introduce a focus of resistance such as suspense/surprise/tension.

End

Resolve the problem, whichever way, and then get out as quickly as possible with the important knowledge that every children's story should end with the *promise of a new beginning*.

Of course, in the *Kyoto* story the 'promise of a new beginning' brings another problem with the oil well. But that is also the start of another story! Crucial to this, though, is the understanding that this is just a very basic formulation. The ideas of Balance, Disharmony and the Inciting Incident can all happen almost immediately in opening the story. For example, if you open the story with a crisis, as I did with *Kyoto*, all this suggests is that prior to this there was Balance which is not worth speaking about. But it's such an easy device:

> Max heard the doorbell ringing a second time. The first time he thought he had been dreaming. He looked at the clock. 'What can anyone want at four o'clock in the morning,' he muttered.

See, it is easy. We are already into the beginning of this thriller. No messing, no thoughts about what he was doing the night before – ring, ring, straight in, where Max has gone on to college and the Wild Things are coming to call (with apologies to Maurice Sendak).

And purely for information, the basic difference between story and plot can be summarised in a few short sentences. A story is a sequence of events, in its most simple form it is usually told in a chronological order and a plot is a means by which the themes, ideas, emotions and dramatic tension and events are arranged. Let's return to an example of *Kyoto*.

- It was a spring morning
- A boy emerges into the sunshine
- A bear emerges into the sunshine
- The boy and the bear slide down the hill and collide
- Suddenly they encounter a problem, the ice is thin and breaks off
- The problem is worse than it looks, they are small people in a huge sea
- The problem is worse, here is an iceberg and a whale

- They land on the shore but the problem is no better
- The problem is worse, there is a monster of machinery and noise
- The problem is worse, they are on a coal mountain
- The solving is dangerous
- The boy takes a chance
- They slide into the sea
- The problem is no better, they are still adrift
- The bear takes a chance and decides to push
- They land on the shore – problem solved
- Lurking in the distance is the shadow of an oil well that had sprung up while they were away.

Simple progress really, but as Nabokov might have said, 'This is the whole story and we might have left it at that had there not been profit and pleasure in the telling . . .' (Nabokov 1936). The series of events listed here are nothing but the cue cards of the story, plotting it for dramatic effect. The writing is where the nuances of the story can be unpicked and embellished and, if a picture book, it is where the images can really take the story forward through the changing scenes. It is all very simple and we can see this idea of a series of events extending the basic tenure of the above charts into six stages of plot development, which can be listed as:

- The opening   The boy and the bear hardly a step from home
- The arrival of conflict   The ice breaks and they slip into the sea
- The early achievement   Out at sea but at least they are safe, if in danger
- The twist and change   Hitting the industrial beach and escaping
- The denouement   Back into the sea and safe for now
- The final outcome   Home

It is often suggested that a story for children should open with conflict but, however minor, the opening has to introduce it. In my own mind, the trick is not to delay the introduction of the conflict too long. Also, this is not a rigid structure but as you can see along the way, from start to finish, there has to be *change*! And Pullman's idea on this is worth noting

> you can't put the plot on hold while you cut artistic capers for the amusement of your sophisticated readers, because, thank God, your readers are not sophisticated. They've got more important things in mind than your dazzling skill with wordplay. They want to know what happens next.[1]

In the end something has to have changed from the beginning, things never go back to being exactly the same as they were. As we can see from this plot model, these six changes are identified as progressive and all of them lead to the mantra – *what happens next*. But don't just take my headings as gospel. Try out your own and see what works for you; also think of variations and ideas on sub-plots, think of introducing other characters even.

But if I were you I would leave out interfering parents – the birth of the child in fiction is the death of the parent. But also do note that the cliché 'he never changes' simply does not hold true. We all change; real life is about changes and change. Your child reader is changing at every reading (if you get more than one) the children (and the bear as a represented child) in *Kyoto* change, they are not the same as they were at the beginning of the story. They saw an opportunity to have fun, they had a wee adventure they hadn't imagined and came unstuck before coming out well at the end. The fact is stories are full of twists and turns; half truths; oxymorons; paradoxes; inconsistencies; absurdity; contradictions; illogical ideas; strangeness; otherness; familiarity; intimacy; formality; informality; knowledge; wisdom; know-how; erudition; culture; learning; and, let's be honest, everything, even the downright daft, where nothing ever stays the same.

Characters

Before I go on to split the *Kyoto* story into two versions, a picture-book version and an early-reader version, it might be worth taking a look at the characters. It is characters that interest us most when we read fiction and it is characters your child reader will be interested in. Think about the interaction between Max and the Wild Things; Peter Pan and Captain Hook; Harry Potter and his friends juxtaposed with 'he who shall not be named'; Pullman's Lyra and Mrs Coulter; indeed Lyra and Iorek Byrnison the armoured bear. The 'what happens next' scenario is almost always about the person in the story: What happened to the girl abducted by aliens? What about the boy who fell into the pond, did his parents mind? Does it matter that the main character is a rabbit who doesn't like lettuce or cabbage? Does it matter that they are Wild Things? Lists like these are endless and ongoing and ever-changing and so they should be. But we can invest so much into making them good, blandness is the death of a character who should literarily sing off the page.

In the *Kyoto* story they have personalities (hopefully) which are defined by their actions and dialogue (or not in the case of the bear). Think about what defines him or her, and where they stand in relation to:

- the story world at large
- the context of the story
- what might be going on in their heads
- what might be going on in the head of others close to them
- what might be real
- what might be imagined
- what might be possible and not
- where they might be going
- what they might say
- what they might do
- what they mean to say to each other (i.e. if the bear can't speak you can inflect on what he might have said by actions)
- what they don't mean to say to each other (i.e. if the bear can't speak you can inflect on what he might have said by actions).

This isn't a tick box, or a check list, it is just a bunch of suggestions in thinking about your character. But important to this, too, is the level of maturity shown by the child. Here I would put both kids in *Kyoto* at around six or seven; old enough to think of life's possibilities while still secure enough from the outside world and societal realities but also old enough for younger, picture-book children to be able to look up to.

But I can also say through this anecdote that thinking about the age of your characters is very important to the readership. Some may disagree and there are instances where exceptions can reveal themselves and it is crucial when thinking about writing for early years children. Even when we are dealing with early years they cannot all fit into the one age-banded demographic because they have varying degrees of experience and maturity. For example, remember what I said in Part I: we need to consider the 3–7 age group highlighted by Nicholas Tucker (Tucker 1981: 46). In the UK, this age grouping manages to collect the following five school categories:

Age 1 to 3   pre-school
Age 3 to 4   nursery
Age 4 to 5   reception
Age 5 to 7   infants
Age 7 +   juniors

Consider then, how important this is. We have to regard these first seven years as probably the most significant learning years of a child's life. It is the period in a child's life when they will learn more than they will ever learn again. You need to consider who this child is. Breaking down the class size isn't a scientific method but at least you have a chance to get a general view of whom you are addressing! Get to know the child! It really does pay to be alert to their picture book and reading needs. Though once again, that's not to say everything can be easily categorised by age alone and if I am repeating myself here then you may get to realise how important it is.

Chapter 14

Picture books illustrated

Before I go into ideas on story and narrative, language and dialogue and rhythm and rhyme in picture books, I need to say something about how they are structured. I said in the previous chapter that a random picture in a picture book stands in isolation but the story relies on the preceding and following pictures for clarity and maintaining the narrative thread. Even the movement from the front cover to the first story page has a context in this. This is really important to the entire construction of the book and to the viability of the story being told.

Picture books are typically 16, 24 or 32 pages long, including two pages for the title and imprint. There is no mystery about this, it's not a crop circle, just the simple fact that this is the way paper is folded for maximum usage and minimum waste. Generally speaking too, 16 pages will be at the lower age range, such as 'board books' for toddlers, and story books in the 24- and 32-page category, although *Magic Mr Edison*, which I mention earlier, is 48 smaller pages because it is intended for school reading as well as general distribution. But taking the average picture book at 32 pages, this leaves you with a minimum of 24 pages, or 12 double spreads, up to a maximum of 30 pages, or 15 double spreads, to work with. And the illustration on page 104 (which I have also used before in Melrose 2002) reveals a typical model for a 32-page book into which we will work *Kyoto* after we have discussed the other issues we have to pay attention to.

As you can see, the 12 double spreads begin on pages 6 and 7 and continue through to pages 28 and 29, although these could be pushed to 13 double spreads with judicious use of the end papers. You can also see from the illustration that it is crucial to consider each single page or each double spread (more usual for this grouping) when you are thinking about the story you are presenting. I like to think of each double spread as a different scene to keep the story moving forward. And opened out this way you really get a chance to plan it out. But think about movement too, read it like a film moving from scene to scene.

One of the best ways to work this too is to mock one up so that you chart the changes. This is crucial to allow you to try to gauge the page-turning ideas, like cliff-hanger page endings and suchlike. And check these against picture books you have access to: you will see from there how this actually works in practice.

But don't think mock-up is just a child's game. It helps you to get hang of the idea that a picture book is about page-turning scenes. Simply take eight pieces of A4 paper and fold them in two to make a 32-page book – voilà. Then enter your text as appropriate, making sure each double spread produces a new scene.

It is important to get this into your head and use the mock-up to try and see your book because a good picture book is not just about a story on a page; as I have written above, it

1	2	3	4	5
End Board	End Paper	End Paper	Prelims	Title Page

6	7	8	9	10	11
Double	spreads	moving	two	by	two

12	13	14	15	16	17

18	19	20	21	22	23

24	25	26	27	28	29

30	31	32
End Paper	End Paper	End Board

Plan for a 32-page picture book – 12 double spreads

is constructed, grown even, to make it accessible and meaningful to a child. Indeed, illustrators, like the talented Ian Beck and Shirley Hughes, always make mock-ups. But what is important to bear in mind when writing is that the illustrator, if not you as writer/illustrator, may end up playing around with your suggested page breaks, and that is something you will have to bear. When it happened to me, and when I was asked to change the text to accompany a really good picture, I did so without hesitation because it wasn't gratuitous fiddling. The illustrator just saw the book differently and it was easy for me to accommodate what she had in mind. But something else happened too. When I saw her interpretive picture, I realised that I should change the text to accommodate the image she was portraying and it was an accommodation that worked very well indeed. At this stage the story I had written had moved on from words on a page to a much more vibrant and visual text. The book was getting made, page by page, illustration by illustration!

How much say you want to have in this process will all depend on your relationship with the publisher and let's not be coy, no one can accommodate every change, it just becomes too costly. Even in a book like this I am constrained and any changes I did make at proof stage were kept to a minimum. Of course it is best to try and get it right first time and let me give you a tip: writing is easy, it's just a question of getting the right words in the right order. Furthermore, the illustrator has to be trusted to visualise your words because he or she is an artist too, only working in a different medium, but to the same end, which is the making of a collaborative piece of art called a picture book.

Taking this chunk of text I will show you how it can be chopped up and edited accordingly, using the model I showed above, with the text reduced to picture book size and standard. The numbers are double spreads:

1

In the coldest country on top of the world, the boy was very happy. It had been a long, dark winter. But today the sun was shining.
He waved goodbye to his mother. Then he yelled, 'Wee . . . ee . . .!' as he dived onto his sledge.

Nearby, a little bear looked happy too. She had been hibernating all winter with her mother. But now it was spring.

Her mother nudged her gently into the snow. Soon the little bear was off exploring.

The yellow sun shone brightly above them.

2

The boy pulled his sledge up the side of a big snow hill.
The little bear climbed up the other side of the hill.
At the top of the hill they both had a brilliant view.

3

Then the boy pushed his sledge down the hill and jumped on board.
Once again he shouted, 'Wee . . . eee . . .!' as he slid down the hill.

The little bear slipped down onto her bottom. She too began to slide down the hill.

4

Down and down and down they slid, slipping and sliding.
The boy couldn't see the little bear.
And the little bear couldn't see the boy.

Suddenly there was an almighty crash.
The boy and the little bear had bumped into each other at the bottom of the hill.

'Oi!' said the boy. And he laughed.
The little bear didn't say anything (because bears can't talk). She just jumped up and shook snow all over the boy.
'Oi!' laughed the boy again.

5

Then something very strange happened. The ground beneath them began to move.
It felt very odd indeed.
The boy and the little bear wobbled from side to side.
They had landed on ice.
The ice trembled and cracked.
Then it broke away and began to float out to sea.

6

At first the waves were gentle.
The ice only bobbled a little.
But suddenly the waves grew bigger and bigger, taking them further and further out
to sea.

Up in the clear blue sky, the sun seemed to shine brighter than ever.

But the boy and the little bear began to feel very dark inside. So they moved closer
together to become friends.

1st Double spread	
In the coldest country on top of the world, the boy was very happy. The long, dark winter had ended.	Nearby, the little bear was looking happy too. She had been hibernating all winter with her mother. But now it was spring. Her mother nudged her gently into the snow.
'Wee . . . ee . . .!' he yelled as he dived onto his sledge.	The yellow sun shone brightly above them.

2nd Double spread	
The boy pulled his sledge up the side of a big snow hill.	The little bear climbed up the other side of the hill.
At the top of the hill they both had a brilliant view.	

3rd Double spread

Then the boy pushed his sledge down the hill and jumped on board.

'Wee . . . eee . . .!' said the boy.

The little bear slipped down onto her bottom.

She too began to slide down the hill.

4th Double spread

Down and down and down they slid, slipping and sliding.

Suddenly there was an almighty crash. The boy and the little bear had bumped into each other at the bottom of the hill.

'Oi!' said the boy. And he laughed.

The little bear didn't say anything (because bears can't talk). She just jumped up and shook snow all over the boy.

'Oi!' laughed the boy again.

As can be seen, I have cut the words right back to the basics, allowing room for the pictures to tell the rest of the story. But it might help to think through the picture ideas too.

1st Double spread[1]

The boy and the bear are both seen leaving home, both mothers look on.

In the bigger context though we can see it is an arctic landscape with a pale yellow sun lighting up the scene and the page.

(In the original this double spread is in colour.)

4th Double spread

This could work as a split screen of smaller pictures telling a whole story:

1. shows the boy sliding down the hill

2. shows the bear sliding separately

3. sees them clashing together and then

4. shows the boy saying 'Oi!' as the bear showers him with snow

What I envisage is the pictures telling a story that crosses over the words narrative, sometimes replicating, sometimes contradicting, especially since boy and the bear don't know each other are there until they collide, whereupon we have our first inciting incident. Although at the end the fictional children still don't know about the oil well. But the readers do because they have seen all the clues and the final, twelfth, double page spread when all is revealed except to the fictional children. It is a bit like the title of this book, *Monsters Under the Bed*, where I envisaged a fictional, picture-book parent saying, 'Go to sleep. There are no monsters under the bed . . .' when you the reader can see the eyes shining and looking up at the speaker. And the whole idea of pictures and words being able to show contradictions and conclusions is really important to cognitive

development. But there is also space to think. Having shown you the pictures on the first pages of the story, it closes with the boy and the little bear's reunion with their parents and then a last double spread which has no words at all, just this illustration. A story in image and the beginning of another story, an ongoing story about global warming which carries on after the book has come to the end. The book is called *Kyoto* – a big story about a boy and a little bear and a little story about global warming.[2]

Chapter 15

Voice and point of view (POV)

The difference between a narrative voice and a point of view (POV) is marked. It would be fair to say that if you read this book cover to cover you might have a narrative voice in your head in which you may think you can hear me speaking. This isn't uncommon but remember when you are writing for young children the voice of the narrator will be a parent or a teacher (for example) and you need to be able to make sure the text sits comfortably to enable it to be read out loud. The alliterative ideas around the 'social significance of serendipitous squeals' might look good on a page but try saying it out loud when there is a child sitting, squealing on your lap. The narrative voice of a picture book and read to book is easily acquired but rehearse it by reading it out loud. If you stumble over your own words then another reader will have no chance. Once while I was sitting in my study writing I heard my daughter, age six, standing outside the door with a school friend. Her friend said, 'What does your dad do in there?' Abbi replied, 'He talks to himself.' Thus, after you have decided on your story, easily one of the most important decisions you will ever make when you begin writing concerns the viewpoint you are going to tell it from. And in doing so you must think about the following – still bearing in mind the young age you are writing for:

*   Who is going to tell the story?
*   Through whose eyes are we told the story?
*   How is the story to be told?
*   Where does the narrator stand in relation to the other characters in the story?
*   What age do you see your characters as being?
*   What level of experience in life do you expect your character to have?
*   How knowing is your character?
*   How lucid is your character?
*   How are you going to create tension between your characters?
*   How do your characters interact with one another?
*   Is there a dominant character in the group?
*   What are the characteristics you wish to imply?
*   Who is going to read the story? This is so very important to all of the above and the reason is a simple one, which I have written of in Part I and which I will repeat below.

The child comes to a story in anticipation of seeing the familiar they recognise and can relate to but also something new they do not know, or may know of but as yet have not articulated. Once again, the child doesn't come to a story for a hidden truth but for what was not there before, prior to their reading of it as part of their experiential development. It is crucial that you address these issues and answer the questions in your own mind.

Then once you have decided on the viewpoint you have to stick to it. The narrative voice must retain an air of familiarity in the constancy of the delivery. A character can't just suddenly change from being Scottish to English unless it's part of a joke or disguise and flagged up early.

'Is yer mammy in?' asked Molly.

'My mammy? Don't you speak funny,' said James.

'I have absolutely no idea what you are talking about,' said Molly in her poshest accent.

Victor Watson (2000) wrote of a child who had explained to him that, 'starting a new novel was like going into a room full of strangers, but starting a book in a familiar series was like going into a room full of friends'. What you will be trying to capture is a sense of familiarity immediately because you will be remembering the picture book/read to book as the mediator in the polysensory experience I mentioned in Part I. And the quotation from Watson sums up a great deal up for me; they are wise words which the writer for early years should heed. It is so important to get the narrative voice into such a good sense of the familiar so that the 'room full of strangers' are the potential new friends. But while the consistency of the voice must be maintained throughout the story it is even more important in a series like *Dilly the Dinosaur* and, to be honest, this is one of the very great things about twenty-first-century children's literature; in my opinion, the writing and publishing standards are extremely high in this respect.

Choosing your narrative voice is important then and it is essential to understand its power. This is especially so in writing for the early years, where changing that narrative voice only leads to confusion. Choose your viewpoint carefully and remember you are not choosing for yourself but for your child who comes to the story with high expectations and it would be a shame to let them down. Now we can move on to viewpoint, which always comes under two very clear headings, called *objective* and *subjective*, but even inside these two headings the variances are very restricted and much narrower than for older through to adult fiction.

Objective viewpoint

The opportunity to use 'objective viewpoint' can come as 'second person' or 'third person'. The second person is where the author uses 'you', as in many songs and poems, guides and some novels, and, of course, non-fiction works such as this book, which has me the writer directly addressing you the reader. The 'third person' is where the author narrates as an outsider, making statements only in the third person. Let me give a couple of examples.

Second person objective is best described as washing machine instructions: First open the door; Second pop in the clothes and the washing powder; Third, turn the dial to . . . etc. In most literature, never mind children's, such use is slight because it relies on a style of reporting where the narrative voice is just a cold delivery of instructions, precluding subjective thinking.

Third person objective is best explained by example. The Prime Minister might think that it is in the interest of our welfare and our joint happiness that we all receive £50 in our Christmas stockings. But he might not say this in a personal voice, preferring to speak on behalf of the metonymy that is the government: 'In the interest of the welfare and joint happiness of the people of the UK, this year the government pledges to deposit £50 in all Christmas stockings' – this being the dull diktat of 'objective' government-speak where the personal has been removed.

The most prominent examples of objective viewpoints are those where the viewpoint is removed from the characters altogether, so that the story's characters, action and speech are simply reported. In this instance, we get to see nothing of their motivation or view of the world they live in. Indeed, most commonly, 'third person objective' is used in mysteries where the motivation of the character needs to remain hidden as part of the mystery. The talented Mr Ripley leaves us wondering: what is *really* going on inside his head as he accepts the serendipitous windfall of every disaster he leaves in his wake? So as you can see, narrative viewpoints or points of view (POV) address a reader directly but this can vary from the personal to the very impersonal and from the subjective to the objective on a sliding scale of knowing and intimacy. As can be seen from this extract of *The Odyssey*, too, the narrator knows the boy Telemachus but gives us very little of his internal thinking:

Book II

Now when the child of morning, rosy-fingered Dawn, appeared, Telemachus rose and dressed himself. He bound his sandals on to his comely feet, girded his sword about his shoulder, and left his room looking like an immortal god. He at once sent the criers round to call the people in assembly, so they called them and the people gathered thereon; then, when they were got together, he went to the place of assembly spear in hand – not alone, for his two hounds went with him. Minerva endowed him with a presence of such divine comeliness that all marvelled at him as he went by, and when he took his place in his father's seat even the oldest councillors made way for him.

(Homer, *The Odyssey*, Trans. Samuel Butler)

The narrator is a fly on the wall character, located at the edge of the narrative and reporting everything that is going on with a matter-of-factness, 'Now when the child of morning, rosy-fingered Dawn, appeared, Telemachus rose and dressed himself.' Who is speaking here? The narrator is kept well outside of the emotional character at all time and we can only guess at the internal thoughts during the scene. Emotion is only reported as witnessed; for example, if he was crying with sadness the narrator would report this. But in this extract, we get no sense of what Telemachus is thinking here and our sense of the story is 'reported' through the actions and words overheard. Thus, this means of writing fails to really explore the emotional depth of the characters. Nevertheless, it does have its uses, for example in picture books for the very young. Let's go back to *Kyoto* for an example.

They floated out to sea. Soon the two friends couldn't see any more land. They passed by a huge iceberg. An enormous whale surfaced to take a look. Then it disappeared again. The boy and the little bear were alone. Floating on the big sea they felt very small indeed. The boy felt cold. But the little bear had her thick fur coat to keep her warm. So she huddled up to the boy to keep him warm too.

After a very long time at sea, the two friends felt the ice wobble again. Then it landed with a bump on a seashore. Both the boy and the little bear jumped onto the beach. They had no idea where they were. Could they be far from home?

It can be very effective as a storytelling device when being addressed through accompanying pictures. And you can see how I have added an authorial intervention inside the narrative voice with the line, 'Could they be far from home?' Indeed, fairy tales are often told this way, especially in 'learning to read' texts, like this example from the British Council.

Little Red Riding Hood is a little girl who lives in a forest! One day she went to visit her granny. Can you guess who she met in the wood?[1]

And you can see how this functions in the narrative. The line, 'Can you guess who she met in the wood?' begs an answer from the child. However the problem is that it's a bit Dr Dryasdust and not terribly exciting. The old chestnut, show-not-tell the story, is preferred more, even in this instance, surely? Personally I find it a little contrived even in learning to read books but then I have always found that reading whole stories is a preferable way to enter the world of reading.

Subjective viewpoint

This is the most common viewpoint in writing for children and the term subject speaks for itself because it allows the writer to write subjective thoughts and allows the reader to get inside their character's head. Which is quite useful, thought Andrew, as he took another sip of Earl Grey tea. Hmm, very useful might be a better way of saying it. He thought on. Oh! the choices. Writing should be easy. After all it is just a case of getting the right words in the right order. But it's like a Mozart opera, there are just too many notes.[2] Usefully, subjective viewpoint comes in three distinct guises.

Omniscient subjective viewpoint

Sometimes called third person unlimited and popularised by the invention of the novel and used widely in the nineteenth century by those golden age, early novelists, George Eliot and Charles Dickens, it is very rarely used these days. I have no immediate knowledge of it in modern children's books at all. Indeed, publishing conventions have all but erased it, so let's get it out of the way quickly. The problem it presents for the reader is that while it presents an omniscient view of the world, everyone's thoughts, feelings, conversations, actions and setting are available too. Every scene is scrutinised and the author tells us everything there is to know but so do the characters as we can get into their heads. But it makes it difficult for a reader to empathise with any given character because the narrative is a collective mass of polyphonic voices all vying for attention, often including the author's omniscient view. The resulting effort is never good for early years children. The narrative voice is bouncing all over the place and has had its day, which really finished in the nineteenth century. But that is not to say when done well it is not effective. Take this example from the beginning of *Daniel Deronda* by George Eliot,

> Was she beautiful or not beautiful? and what was the secret of form or expression which gave the dynamic quality to her glance? Was the good or the evil genius dominant in those beams? Probably the evil; else why was the effect that of unrest rather than of undisturbed charm? Why was the wish to look again felt as coercion and not as a longing in which the whole being consents?
>
> (Eliot 1876: 1)

Of which Sally Shuttleworth talked about in terms of where 'the comfort of certainty must be exchanged for an openness to the unknown' (Shuttleworth 1984: 176). It can be seen how this method could work in a picture-book setting, though not in short fiction for children.

First person

Children do, indeed, like reading first person narratives and the reason is simple, it is the first point of view we all identify with. Even if we begin learning to write with what is essentially an 'objective viewpoint', we tend to develop the subjective through the first person and the pronoun 'I'. Our first writing comes from our own personal point of view; we think in the personal; we address the world from a personal perspective when we are telling a story and when we are formulating our own stories we began by involving ourselves, so how would a child not be able to identify with it? But this never works in picture books. It doesn't work because the child being read to cannot identify with the 'I' character – and I explained this at length in Part I. But for an early reader it can be perfect, as in the example of *Dilly the Dinosaur* I used earlier. But let's look at *Kyoto* again.

> 'Hey look at you. You have coal dust all over your face. It makes you look more like a panda than a polar bear.' I was laughing. But then I saw I had upset the little bear. I didn't mean to be cruel. I couldn't help it. She did look like a panda.
>
> 'Here,' I said, 'let me wipe your face. Mum won't mind if I get my jacket dirty. Not when I tell her why.'

Because the narrator addresses the reader directly, using the pronoun 'I', the reader is drawn into a textual collusion with the narration, which is delivered from the boy's point of view. Unlike hearing the story being told the process is internalised and the narrative is inclusive. This is especially the case when we are dealing with older fiction, where issues are dealt with as questions straight from the internal thoughts of the protagonist – i.e., putting onto paper those thoughts we never share or hear shared in real life. But it works for younger fiction too as we saw in the wonderful *Dilly the Dinosaur* series. The narrative is given through the eyes of Dilly's sister, Dorla. And while it is a quite brilliant example of good, subtle, first person narrative, for the younger reader, the empathy of the 'sister' in that family unit is ever-present. But that doesn't mean it is a simple little narrative, it's actually quite complex in structure with a number of positives and negatives wrestling for sense, as this short passage with its extended sentences and ellipses reveals:

Usually at the weekend we have to go shopping, and that is something I hate. It isn't that I don't like looking round big stores . . . I do. I particularly like to look at the toys and books. But what I don't like is that every time we go shopping, Dilly is bound to be bad.

(Bradman 1987: 38)

Third person limited

This, along with first person, is the most common point of view used in children's and indeed most fiction. It is a very effectual approach and probably the simplest to negotiate. Basically what happens is the entire story is written from the perspective of the main character. Children especially like this approach because it allows them to progress from the first person pronoun 'I' to thinking more of others in the story narrative. The technique allows them to empathise completely with the character you have created for them (presuming, of course, the character deserves their empathy), so let's show how it works.

Suddenly the little bear looked frightened as a loud, scary noise roared behind her.

'Look out!' said the boy. He managed to pull her back just in time. A huge coal lorry thundered past them. Then another and another!

'Phew!' said the boy to the little bear. 'That was close!' He had never seen such monster lorries before.

Then more lorries sped towards them.

The boy was thinking, we have to get out of here. But the little bear was already trying to run away.

But they were too late. A huge digger scooped them up with the coal and dumped them right on top of the coal mountain. Then the digger dumped more coal beside them. Then it dumped more coal and more coal, again and again.

The monster lorries and dumping diggers and smoking chimneys and the noisy factory machines rattled and clanged. This is scary, thought the boy. But he didn't want to say it out loud in case it frightened the little bear even more.

What we read is the 'dumping on the coal mountain' scene and it can be very effective in raising the tension. But as you can see all the subjective thoughts remain with the boy. In a refinement of this technique we can informalise it even more to excellent effect, so that it's only a whisper away from first person.

The boy couldn't sleep on the iceberg. It wasn't because he was cold. The little bear was keeping him warm. But it was because he was scared. Mum and Dad must be missing him.

It could be argued that this is mixing third and first person viewpoint but it has a persuasive quality to it and for the child reader the informal naming of 'Mum and Dad' rather than using the formal, 'his mum and dad' brings the narrator closer. It is only a variant on the technique but the intimacy is implicit and immediate. It takes us much closer to the main character without having to rely on the restrictive and often self-important inflection of *me, myself, I* when using the first person. For me the best exponent of this is Louis Sachar in *Holes* (2000).

Third person unlimited

Like omniscient subjective, this is another option which you will never use for children. It will mean all of the voices having subjective thoughts too and it is just far too confusing. Indeed, not since the big fat novels of the nineteenth century like *Middlemarch* has it been used to any great effect and to write that way now would anachronistic. That's not to say it couldn't work in a hypertext kind of way but it is not recommended for any child reader.

Hopefully, then, you have managed to make some sense of viewpoint. The crucial point is make the narrative clear. Choose your viewpoint carefully, then make it strong and make it interesting. To paraphrase what I have written in Part I, your reading child has already come to the story with some ideas of their own even if his or her silence is a hypothetical postulate full of thoughts and thinking, which is always expressed in ellipses . . . where the unsaid and unsayable does not mean the unknown (for the child's time being) because the language, the point of view, the narrative voice you use to express knowledge comes after, through ageing and experience (lived in and lived out) and is gained, minute by minute, second by second, both primarily and vicariously, in the child's ongoing development.

Chapter 16

Dialogue, rhythm and rhyme

You may have noticed that what I have established above in the *Kyoto* story is that a lot of writing for children is undertaken through the use of dialogue. This is very important in writing for early years. It is important that a child begins to develop their own vocabulary and dialogue helps them to understand that discourse is wider than just their thoughts and words. Of course, this goes well beyond books and films. As I wrote in *Here Comes the Bogeyman*, language is not merely given by an adult to a child, but gained by the child in many and multicultural ways[1] and the reading child being addressed by the book can already understand more than she or he can articulate, especially as they become readers – and this becomes a defining issue which I will repeat in isolation because it's very important to record it.

~~ Children understand more than they can articulate at all the stages of their life ~~

Their articulation comes through dialogic[2] social and cultural negotiation and a journey through phonology, vocabulary, morphology and syntax, not as a list to tick off but as a dialogic part of growing up and this is as it should be. Dialogic dialogues are a way of allowing the writer to represent self-consciously aware characters, such as the boy represented in *Kyoto*, as being able to speak for themselves. And this is immensely important in children's fiction. Allowing the child to 'speak' in a text is extremely important. Granted, it is still your 'adult imported ideas' but remember what I said before about the writer and the reader 'exploring' the options.

The important thing to remember here is the imagined child being read to/reader at the other end of the creative chain begins with you writing. I as the 'real author' am writing to you as an 'implied reader' and you the 'real reader' are only engaging with me as the 'implied author'. You are the reader I imagine and I am the writer you imagine and along the way we may never meet (sadly). Writing for children is no different, you have to be able to imagine your reader. But crucial to this is the fact that your reader is also imagining you, so it is a reciprocal exploration of the text.

Before I move on I want to address another issue for you as a writer to consider. I want to show some dialogue between two then three characters called Cait, Tom and Meerah, so but let's take it a step at a time by sidelining Meerah for now:

> The sky was still dark but the rain had finally stopped.
> 'What a storm that was last night. Did you hear it,' said little Tom.
> Cait nodded, she had heard it. It had kept her dog Zakkie awake. She had heard him howling every time there was thunder and lightning. 'Yes, I heard it. And Zakkie howled all night.'

'Did, he?' asked Tom. 'I never heard him. Once I am asleep I stay sleeping.'

How could he not have heard it thought Cait. She yawned. 'I don't think I slept all night.'

'Actually, me neither,' said Billy, who liked to do and say everything Cait did. 'I was only pretending I slept.'

Cait just smiled. She knew Billy too well by now. 'Let's go down into the garden,' she said.

The dialogue between two people is generally more intimate than, say, when there are more involved. But the options are restricted, A talks to B and B talks to A, back and forth. As you can see the dialogue exchange possibilities are restricted.

Introducing another voice doesn't just make a threesome it introduces the factor three to the equation and gives six options. See the diagram below:

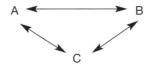

The sky was still dark but the rain had finally stopped.

'What a storm that was last night. Did you hear it,' said little Tom.

Cait nodded, she had heard it. It had kept her dog Zakkie awake. She had heard him howling every time there was thunder and lightening. 'Yes, I heard it,' she said. 'And Zakkie howled all night.'

'Did he?' asked Meerah. 'I never heard a thing. Once I am asleep I stay sleeping.'

How could she not have heard it thought Cait. She yawned. 'I don't think I slept all night.'

'Me neither,' said Billy, who liked to do everything Cait did.

Cait just smiled. She knew Billy too well by now.

'Yes you did, Tom. I heard you snoring away. He came into my room to sleep on the bottom bunk because he was scared of the storm,' said Meerah to Cait.

'No I didn't,' said Billy.

Cait just laughed. 'Let's go down into the garden,' she said.

As you can see with this alternative, A can speak to B and C, B can speak to A and C and C to A and B. Thus the potential to open the dialogue out and widen the subject matter, give facts, etc., is easier to manage. But it also also allows us to play with tension and play characters off against each other. See how Meerah sidelines Tom in a knowing, teasing conversation with Cait, at Tom's expense. Now looking at the normative ideas on age-related discourse, we can see how the narrative can manipulate the characters very simply. Cait and Meerah are capable of ganging up on Tom, although he will soon get his own back and this isn't showing Meerah as cruel, just realistic. Also, as we can see, the dialogue is best kept brief and each word weighted to moving the scene and the story forward. Elizabeth Bowen offers some excellent advice on this (cited in Boulter 2007: 155):

1. dialogue should be brief
2. it should add to the reader's present knowledge
3. it should eliminate the routine exchanges of ordinary conversation
4. it should convey a sense of spontaneity but eliminate the repetitiveness of real talk
5. it should keep the story moving forward
6. it should be revelatory of the speaker's character, both directly and indirectly it should show the relationships among people.

Look at this checklist in relation to the small snatch of story dialogue I supplied and look for the links. In the words of Frey, 'dialogue should be in conflict, indirect, clever, and colourful' (Frey 1987: 114). And this is not hard to achieve, as I have demonstrated.

Rhythm and rhyme

It is also worth bearing in mind that a mock-up helps you to work out the pace and rhythm of the work, thinking about page turning and rhythmic patterns. Before I go on to explain this, though, we need to consider rhyme. It is a simple fact that when it is done right and well in a picture book rhyming can be wonderfully good. I cite *Room on the Broom* written by Julia Donaldson[3] and illustrated by Axel Scheffler (2002) as an exemplar. Here is the first sentence:

> The witch had a cat
> and a very tall hat,
> and long ginger hair
> which she wore in a plait.

And also, from the dark little book, *Mouse Look Out* written by Judy Waite and illustrated by Norma Burgin (1988):

> Then silent as the sunset,
> a shadow came creeping.
>
> MOUSE, LOOK OUT,
> THERE'S A CAT ABOUT!

In both cases the rhyme is important to the rhythm of the narrative and to the visual flow but this comes with a huge caveat. The fact is publishers would prefer not to get strict rhyming text unless it's really really good. The fact is that such texts are hard to get into co-editions. And I know it's hard to accept but market forces sometimes have to be considered if you wish your book to be published internationally. If you have ever undertaken a literal translation from German into English you will see why.

Nevertheless, that does not mean you cannot be poetic in the language you use, as Waite shows in her 'silent as the sunset a shadow came creeping'. The alliterative and sibilant **S** in 'silent as the sunset a shadow . . .' quickly followed by the alliterative hard **C** consonants in '. . . came creeping . . .' has a poetic quality to it. But you will see the Donaldson text is different, it has a very strict rhyming scheme which is rhythmic and works in a similar way to nursery rhymes. For example, I love the improper 'looking' rhyme in the words hat and plait. It looks improper on the page but is a proper rhyme when spoken, which is to say it is a feminine rhyme by appearance and a masculine rhyme by sound, so it's a hermaphrodite rhyme which I have seen called an apocopated rhyme. Plait, as everyone should know is pronounced *plat* and this just adds to the fun of the picture book. But if strict rhyming is generally frowned upon, having some poetic ideas is very welcome. In *Magic Mr Edison* (2002: 18) I used the phrase,

> Charlie knocked over a fruit cart.
> Apples and pears rolled everywhere.

And the improper rhyming link between 'pears' and 'everywhere' is just a little nudge in the poetic language direction and it works quite well in creating a rhythmic effect. So think about these things too because picture books are about representation and about language but also about reading out loud. And as I have already shown, in *Kyoto* I wrote, 'Oi! Said the boy'. In a read to text these little things come as icing to the language cake without overloading it with cherries on top, as those last words I have just written clearly do to this sentence. The trick is not to overdo it.

Furthermore, as can be seen, the rhythm is just as important as the rhyme and do check this out. How many books have you seen that just roll off the tongue with a constant, undulating rhythm. Just like a good song, it needn't rhyme but can it move along in time to a heartbeat, which is four/four time. If your heart and the rhythm of your prose is beating seven/eight you are hitting a dissonant wall, either that or you are stumbling along without giving the rhythm too much thought. Go back to what I said about the picture book process also being about nurture and the polysensory event, where heartbeat is important and good rhythm is more essential than a clumsy rhyme and indeed sometimes more important than the actual words. My daughter once asked me to play the 'butter song' with her. We sat on the floor and sang while playing holding hands and rowing, and it went like this,

> Row, row, row the boat,
> gently down the stream,
> merrily, merrily, merrily, merrily,
> life is butter dream (*but a dream*)

And *butter dream* it remained! It is not a hugely critical or scientific analysis but you can see why the rhythm was so much more important in the game that accompanies this song. Besides, what child could understand the phrasing of the words, 'life is but a dream'? Who nowadays speaks thus? I know not, but anachronism is not an easy word to say in a picture book situation, neither is narcissistic or discombobulated, although I rather like discombobulated because it has a humorous, childish charm to it.

Word count

The wordiness of picture books varies greatly. I have seen anything from a word a page to around fifteen hundred words. For a younger age group the word count is usually on the low side. This is easily researched too. I recently revisited two old favourites in our house. *Jasper's Beanstalk*, by Nick Butterworth and Mick Inkpen has only ninety-two words and

Mouse Look Out, by Judy Waite, has 403 words. Yet both tell equally relevant stories and stand on the same experiential picture-book shelf as exemplary stories. But if you are thinking about getting your story over around 800–850 words you might be targeting the wrong medium and are actually beginning to write an early reader as opposed to a picture book. But the secret is that there is no secret. Simply go to a library or a book shop and check them out. Everyone should research when they are writing and a book like this might send out good messages but you have to get out into the world and check for yourself.

Chapter 17

Story

Now then, you may be wondering why I dealt with so many issues first, such as characters, voice and dialogue, when I had said the most important thing would be story. Well, the answer is I simply wanted to get it out of the way. It is the factual stuff you need to know about. It is also the 'objective' stuff you can check and compare; what it doesn't do is talk about the 'subjective' and, believe me, that is much harder. It took me about two hours to write *Magic Mr Edison* and about a month to settle on a final draft – and even then we were tweaking right up to the last minute, which was about a year down the line from starting. Do not be fooled into thinking these are just little stories. They are not, they are big stories told short and there is a huge difference. All early years children are young and inexperienced but the stories can be very sophisticated indeed, as we can see with *Where the Wild Things Are*.

Einstein for children, did I hear you ask? OK, Einstein is sitting with a child on the sofa and the child, age four, say, asks the great man to explain the great theory he keeps talking about. 'Ah,' said Einstein, 'you must mean the theory of relativity. Well, it is really quite simple. If you were sitting on this sofa and playing with your best friend, two hours can seem like two minutes. But if you were sitting with a boring old coot like me, two seconds can seem like two hours.' Voilà! OK, I adapted Aiden Chambers' version (Chambers 1985: 60) but that's fine. T. S. Eliot said, 'Immature poets imitate; mature poets steal . . .' and I don't think I defaced the story by making it child-accessible. But Chambers does make a hugely relevant point when he says,

> Relativity has changed our ideas about time, space, cause and effect. That old definition of Story, *what happens to whom and why*, is having to change in order to accommodate extra elements into the formula: the elements, *where, when,* and *seen by whom?* Relativity requires that we look at everything from more than one point of view.
>
> (Chambers 1985: 60–1)

This is something that can vary. The aim of every picture book is to present a complete and coherent idea in as few words as possible. Every single word must count. Avoid any unnecessary padding, whimsy and off-hand comments because most of this can be conveyed through the pictures if they enhance the story. Make every word count in driving the story forward. The story has to move from page to page, each page leading to the next and anticipating the next page to come. And remember, too, it has to be a story. I know for a fact that publishers are tired of writers sending them lists of events which become more like a child's story rather than a story for a child – and you must be aware of the difference. As Nodelman writes,

> the mere fact that it [a picture book] is told over a number of pages broken up by pictures forces a picture-book narrative to tend toward the strong rhythmic beat of pictures in sequence. Stories consisting of small segments of separate activity lack the continuity and the suspense we identify with good storytelling.
>
> A good picture-book text not only contains the wider variety of sentences we might expect but also uses the pauses created by the presence of pictures more imaginatively.
>
> (Nodelman 1988: 249)

Also, allow the pictures room to complement the text. Think about what I said in Part I about the idea of pictures coming to be grouped into complementary, symmetry, enhancement, counterpoint and contradiction, with the inevitable leakage across them.

The best gift a writer can give is space for the illustrator to work his or her own magic in the text. The result is worth the extra effort for the child because the story is a combined story of text and image, not two separate parts of the same book. And picture/text balance can only be accomplished if the text is kept sparse, avoiding filling in the detail that the picture can cover. A phrase such as, 'the wind howled' is sufficient for an illustrator to conjure up a huge double spread of images and off the top of my head I am thinking:

- an old lady hanging onto her hat while her umbrella is turned inside out
- a newspaper blowing down the street
- waves crashing over the pier
- huge billowing clouds racing across the sky
- trees bending low in the unforgiving wind
- leaves blowing everywhere
- a child clinging to a tree, legs in the air and about to be sucked away.

How can we 'see' the wind? Well, we get the picture, don't we? This list could go on and on as a potential visual image with no words necessary.

But what words you do use are very important. While the text is short it has to be able to stand alone as a complete story. No illustrator, however great, will ever be able to make up for an inadequate or mediocre narrative. Keep sentences short and simple so the pictures can breathe life into them. Also keep the sentences short and simple because the text has to be read out loud. It should also be remembered that such books have more than one storyteller: one is the writer of the story, another is the illustrator a third is the reader of the story, fourth is the central charcter who leads the story into what happens next and finally there is the child receiving it because he or she is not a 'passive' recipient but an 'active' explorer.

But, crucially, it is the book's *concept* which comes to dominate. If the concept is right the words and pictures will soon follow. And don't think the concept needs to be that simple, either. Judy Waite's book, *Mouse Look Out*, won the English Association's prize for the best picture book of 1999 but it is a very dark story about an exploring mouse being tracked by a cat, who doesn't see the dog behind it. Never think children are frightened off by challenging text, the only thing that scares them off is a bad story. And indeed we can return again to the Maurice Sendak/Art Spiegelman conversation I referred you to above. Art Spiegelman was talking about his own (wonderful) *Maus*, which is about Auschwitz, and he said that he thought people who gave the book to their children were committing child abuse, to which Sendak replied, 'Art – you can't protect kids … they know everything!' (cf. Zornado 2001: 172–3). Of course there has to be some leeway and judgement here and I don't think anyone can dictate. I tend to take the Judith Kerr line in *When Hitler Stole Pink Rabbit* (2008) and *My Henry* (2011); difficult subjects can be addressed easily enough, if you approach them with care and attention.

Space (in)between

I know I have addressed this in Part I but its crucial to keep it in mind, so I am repeating it here but with some context on the *Kyoto* story. Allowing the book to become a component part of the experiential child's exploring life alongside 'the giants', as I labelled them earlier, is the big challenge of the book if it is to mediate the in-between space. Look at this again, as I discussed in the critical Part I, in a reciprocal, shared experience the book becomes the mediator, as this simple diagram reveals:

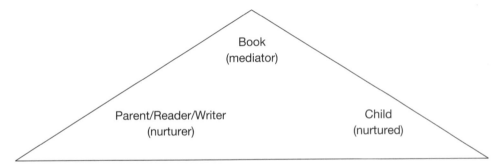

As mediator in an experience shared by both adult and child the book is a huge and important psychological and sociological tool. Rather than thinking of this as a diagram, think about it as an actual experience, think about it being a reader/parent (for example) on a sofa with an arm around the child while both of them engage with the book, one reading the other looking at the pictures and listening to the words.[1]

As I mentioned before, Walter Benjamin might have referred to this as the embodiment of the trading of experiences, the *Erfahrung*, where the shift between 'lived through' and 'narratable experience' is seen as a point of arbitration and negotiation, an exploration of ideas. Try to think of this text in terms of astonishment, intimacy and making the connections and as Benjamin also suggested, connect the words and images which are like the fragments of a vessel that make up the narrative, 'in order to be articulated together [they] must follow one another in the smallest details although they need not be like one another'. It is also important to remember that astonishment, intimacy and making the connections is something we never lose, surely? Also, though for young children, think about the last time you visited the cinema or watched television, you may have noticed that the action taking place is not explained through the dialogue. Rather, the picture and dialogue combine to create an overall impression. The same goes for the

picture book. But, generally, at the simpler end of the scale the clues and connections are more obvious.

In the *Kyoto* story I gave as an example, there were adult-related clues throughout with the images of the oil drilling and the coal mines and the smoke and soot etc. in the industrial town. These are introduced to encourage dialogue and future understanding. But there are other adult considerations present too, which are not quite so obvious, that is clear, and it would be fair to take Nodelman's point that, 'Something might well be identified as nonchildlike or beyond the ken of childlike consciousness [in a cultural product for children] . . .' which reveals the 'hidden adult' (Nodelman 2008: 206). But far from being some huge and hidden secret that adult sensibility haunts such a narrative, for me the 'adult' presence in an 'adult, child-centred' cultural product is ever-present and, in fact, far from being hidden it is the elephant in the room. Indeed, this narrative misses what critics for decades have been trying to establish since Jacqueline Rose's by-now famous quotation:

> Children's fiction is impossible, not in the sense that it cannot be written (that would be nonsense), but in that it hangs on an impossibility, one which rarely speaks. This is the impossible relation between adult and child . . . Children's fiction is clearly about

the relation [between adult and child], but it has remarkable characteristics of being about something which it hardly ever talks of. Children's fiction sets up a world in which the adult comes first (author, maker, giver) and the child comes after (reader, product, receiver), *but where neither of them enter the space in between* [my italics].

(Rose 1984: 1–2)

Using this argument, the fact is that if we do not explore the 'space in-between', adult produced, child-centred cultural product simply conceals the 'hidden child' who is initially invisible to us because we are not children too. But if we begin to understand that children do not come to a book, or a film, or a play, or a contemporary artistic event as a passive 'other' but as an active participatory, albeit less experienced, thinking, human being then we get closer to recognising him or her. And also closer to recognising that the 'space in-between' is the site for astonishment, intimacy and connections being explored by the adult and the child in the process.

It is to be hoped the wider context and concept of the *Kyoto* story (for example) allows the child to see the cause, effect and consequence of certain, seemingly innocuously, playful actions. But the paucity of narrative, linked to the picture, allows the cognitively developing child to understand that words alone do not tell the whole story. And I repeat something I have written above, children can understand much more than they can articulate or express.

I am also persuaded by George Orwell's rules for writing in this respect too. He wasn't talking about picture books but he might well have been – I have added my own thoughts inside the square brackets.

1. Never use a metaphor, simile or other writing figure of speech which you are used to seeing in print [avoid them like the plague].
2. Never use a long word when a short one will do [scatological jokes are pants].
3. If it is possible to cut out a word, always cut it out [the sea was icy . . . see 1 above].
4. Never use the passive when you can use the active [Wee . . . ee . . .].
5. Never use a foreign phrase, a scientific word or a jargon word if you can think of an everyday English equivalent [it was George Bush who said the trouble with the French is they have no word for *entrepreneur*].
6. Break any of these rules sooner than say anything outright barbarous [I mentioned the book, *Go the F**k to Sleep* earlier, didn't I? The point of which I still do not see – *sacré bleu* he says in *Franglais*!].

(Orwell 2000: 359)

As Amanda Boulter comments,

He [Orwell] acknowledges that 'one could keep all of them and still write bad English' (p. 359) but these are good rules to keep in mind as a writer, because if you flout them, you must justify it to yourself when you are editing, asking yourself is it stylistically vital or simply laziness.

(Boulter 2007: 88)

On this issue of story, a good thing to think about for this age is the 'rule of three', cue *Goldilocks and the Three Bears* etc. The symmetry of three, coinciding with beginning, middle and end, keeps the heightened tension of the story going forward. There is little chance of the story sagging if the quest is concluded only after the third attempt, for example and, indeed, early failure is developmental in terms of character and plotting. How does your character respond to failure? To give up loses the story, to persevere is dramatic and allows the child to begin to understand how the story process works. Of course, repetitions in threes in the text work too, 'I'll huff and I'll puff and I'll blow your house down,' works well in *The Three Little Pigs*. And we can see how an extension of this works very well in *We Are Going on a Bear Hunt*, which we discussed above. These five lines are repeated throughout the book and once the journey to the bear is complete the narrative is repeated as the story is then told in reverse as they all return home.

> We're going on a bear hunt.
> We're going to catch a big one.
> What a beautiful day!
> We're not scared.
> Oh-oh!

> (Rosen 1989)

Repetition allows the child to visit and revisit the ideas being presented – who's been sitting in my chair?

Once you have this story, go through it again and again and again, look to revise and rewrite it, believe me it will need it! I said earlier, try and make a little mock-up. This helps us to see the page turning as part of the storytelling process. But it is very important to read it out loud. This will help you to locate any clumsy writing, loose alliteration, dodgy rhythm, creaky sentences, lost sense and nonsense. Better still, record yourself on your mobile phone and then play it back, listening for those rough edges. Then even better still, get someone else to read it out loud to you. When you hear it read back as it appears on the page, rather than with your *imagined* inflection and delivery it can be a real shock – but what a good exercise in editing it is.

Chapter 18

Early readers

Stepping beyond the picture book into the early-reader stage is not a huge leap but it is a very important one because it can be the start of the rest of a child's life, opening up a whole new and huge world. One of the first things we have to think about is the movement away from pictures to books with the odd line drawing here and there. But while the language of the picture book is kept deliberately simple and fairly precise, as I revealed above, at the early-reader stage we can begin to introduce a simile and perhaps even a small metaphor without having to rely on the illustration to support it. But let's remind ourselves of something about story. Tony Burgess asks, 'What happens when we tell a story and why do we do it?' He answers the question himself:

> Most of us, perhaps, tell stories of some kind daily – out of our own need, or for our own and other people's pleasure. Sometimes these stories are about ourselves (at their simplest about what we have been doing), sometimes about others (for the interest of our audience in a mutual acquaintance). What the listener is generally interested in is how the world appears to another person. When the story illuminates that, we are close to fiction.
>
> (in Meek, Warlow and Barton 1977: 363)

The *Kyoto* story lends itself to the picture book style because of its reliance on the images and pictures to support the darker elements of the story and the text struggles to maintain that in its present form – which would be pared back even further as the pictures developed. But I can still use it to explain certain ideas and techniques to you. On the idea of simile and metaphor, for example,

> They had been afloat for a long time when the little bear jumped up. She seemed to be staring at something. Then suddenly she jumped into the sea.
> 'Oi!' said the boy. He didn't want to be left alone. 'It's as cold as ice in there.'
> But the boy wasn't being left alone. Bears are very good swimmers and the little bear was pushing the sledge.
> The sea gave a mighty sigh. The little bear kicked her legs with all her strength. The floating sledge flew across the blue water. At last there was a bump and the sledge scraped onto the seashore.
> This new land looked familiar to the boy. Everything looked normal.
> The boy and the little bear jumped onto the ice and looked up the shoreline
> The boy's mother waved at him.

The little bear's mother roared.

'Where have you been?' asked the boy's mother.

He looked over at his friend. 'Looking after the little bear . . .' The little bear looked back at the boy, '. . . and she was looking after me!' he said.

The little bear didn't say anything (because bears can't talk).

The simile is easy to spot it is *cold as ice* (and a bit of a cliché, which can be a breathe of fresh air to a child, although I tend to avoid them like the plague) but the small metaphorical sea sighing and the bear who makes the sledge float and fly across the water works too. So too the little rhyme '. . . *flew* across the *blue* water' and, once again, "Oi!' said the boy'. Linking the metaphor to the initial simile is not pushing the child's reading too hard. Also, the children are being opened up to an image and an idea with only minimal pictorial intervention, while also being faced with the pleasure of reading as story for themselves. But note, too, the sentences are short and crisp. An adult reader could quite easily get this moving much quicker.

These issues are all actually fairly clear here because the reading age of the child is aligned to their experience. At age four children are still being read to, although they are beginning to read aloud to parents and also beginning to pick up books for reading themselves. However, by the time they are seven (and if everything is going to plan, literacy-wise) they should be capable of reading short novels for themselves. So there is a big age and ability spread here. But it is not too difficult to discern.

The books they will be engaging with are short novels or collections of stories; classic examples of collections are the *Horrid Henry* stories by Francesca Simon or *My Little Sister* by Dorothy Edwards. The text, while still simple like the picture book, can be slightly more sophisticated and you have a larger word-count in which to tell the story. But the inspiration and source of the story can be huge. Bruno Bettelheim, in *The Uses of Enchantment*, wrote:

> Since ancient times the near-impenetrable forest in which we get lost has symbolised the dark, hidden, near-impenetrable world of our unconscious . . . In his dark forest the fairy-tale hero often encounters the creation of our wishes and anxieties – the witch – who would not have the power of the witch . . . and use it to satisfy all his desires, to give him all the good things he wishes for himself . . .? And who does not fear such powers if some other possesses them and might use them against him?
>
> (Bettelheim 1976: 94)

Think about it! Is this not the essence of a good novel for children? The empowering or fight against the abuse of power. Think of the forest as a metaphor (that word again) for that which lurks in the great story box, where all unwritten stories lie in wait. And then consider the possibilities because this metaphorical forest can be anything we like.

One thing to guard against though is that the story still has to be economical. Don't let the increased word-count fool you. If you merely fill it up with descriptive prose or delays that go nowhere, your story will go nowhere. Take this example:

> The boy had been awake all morning. He was thinking about his new sledge and all the wonderful adventures he had planned. It had been a long cold winter. But now it was spring there would be nothing to stop him. It was especially good that school

didn't start for another two weeks. No algebra or arithmetic to take up all his time. He was free to do whatever he wanted.

The problem with this is it is just lying around. Nothing is happening, Apart from telling us he is looking forward to getting outside it's all fairly pointless and just eating up words. Let's get him out there and into the story straight away.

> In the coldest country on top of the world, the boy was very happy. It had been a long, dark winter. But today the sun was shining.
> He waved goodbye to his mother. Then he yelled, 'Wee . . . ee . . .!' as he dived onto his sledge.
> Nearby, the little bear was looking happy too. She had been hibernating all winter with her mother. But now it was spring.
> Her mother nudged her gently into the snow. Soon the little bear was off exploring.

Get straight into the story without hanging around. Look too at the informality of the language in the text, with onomatopoeic, single-word expressions, like, 'wee . . . ee . . .' instead of something more formal. This helps to accentuate the sense of realism. Because we have to remember that enunciation and pronunciation don't quite follow good grammar rules when spoken out loud.

Length: If I were to use the *Kyoto* story as an early reader rather than a picture book, I would probably write four stories for a single collection, using the same characters and each story would be around fifteen-hundred words. So the book would come in at around five to six thousand words and fifty pages (ish). Which is also what an early-reader novel would come in at too (see below).

Chapters: these are one of the most rewarding things a new reader can ever be offered. The sense of achievement is massive. But strange as it may seem, there has to be a sense of regulation to this, a discipline. And think about this for yourself: if you are going to read a book before going to bed, for example, peeling off a couple of chapters is easier if they are roughly the same length and consistency. This comes at an early age and the new reader should not have to plough through thousands of words just to get to the end of a chapter. Making chapters too long kills the incentive before they have even started. Split the chapter book up evenly: five thousand words fits ten chapters quite nicely and it's roughly forty pages. I was writing a series of short novels once and the remit I had was for roughly thirteen thousand words, thirteen–fourteen chapters, so you can see I was heading for around nine-hundred to a thousand words a chapter. It is not rocket science this. But it is important.

So, too, is the idea that each chapter has to have its own beginning, middle and end, and especially useful is ending with a cliff-hanger that encourages the early reader to read on to want to find out 'what happens next'. Remember, the book is competing with many distractions for a child who does not have a huge attention span. Finding out what happens next has to be worth waiting on.

Dialogue: see the examples in the section above. Dialogue is *very* important to the text but it is not chit-chat. It is all about taking the story forward and what is crucial is the information it imparts. For example,

Tom was trying to reach the bananafish with his net.

'It's too short,' said Meerah. 'You'll never reach it from there.'

Tom was disappointed. But he didn't want to go too close. He was a little scared the bananafish might jump up and pinch his nose. But he did want to catch it.

'I have an idea,' said Cait. 'Tom, why don't you climb up the apple tree and reach down? You'll be much closer there.'

Sitting up the tree, Tom looked down. 'This is better. I am right above it.'

'Go on, Tom! Catch it,' shouted Meerah.

As you can see the action taking place is not being described by the children. It is being told through a combination of their talking and short snippets of descriptive action. But even this can be improved upon by looking at the perspective and thinking about the viewpoint as being more than just a point of view but as a special consideration.

Viewpoint is important and I have already discussed it, but extend the idea beyond first person and third person into how you are presenting a view of the world through the eyes of the fictional characters you have written. This is not a world viewed from an adult perspective but from less experienced and smaller people. If I stand up and look at the books on my shelf I can see them at eye level but an early-reader child would be looking up at them. So their sense of perspective is different, they see the world from a completely different viewpoint. Let's go back. Tom was trying to reach the bananafish with his net.

'It's too short,' said Meerah. 'You'll never reach it from there.'

Tom was disappointed. But he didn't want to get too close. He was a little scared he would fall in. He was also scared the bananafish might jump up and pinch his nose. But he did want to catch it.

'I have an idea,' said Cait. 'Tom, why don't you climb up the apple tree and reach down? You'll be much closer there.'

Tom looked up at the tree. It was higher than anything he had climbed before. 'It's too tall,' he said.

'No it's not,' said Cait. She pointed, 'Look that branch is nearly touching the water. You could reach from there.'

The tree still looked tall to little Tom. 'Well, I could try,' he said, bravely.

What I have done is adjust the perspective to make Tom look smaller and the task harder. You have to think of the view of the world and the perspective being presented. Little Tom has to climb up the tall tree and look down. So the whole idea of perspective points to his size. In *Kyoto* it's the same,

Soon the two friends couldn't see any more land.

They passed by a huge iceberg. An enormous whale surfaced to take a look.

Then it disappeared again.

The boy and the little bear were alone.

Floating on the big sea they felt very small indeed.

What I have done is adjust the perspective to make the boy and the bear look even smaller and the task harder. Simply just giving the narrative the easy route isn't enough.

Plot: stories this length do not have fantastic scope for plotting but they still need to have a beginning, middle and ending and while the plot is simple to provide only for a faint sub-plot, the texture of the story has to be altered slightly to accommodate what the pictures could replace. I have already given this information before (Melrose 2002) but since I invented this and it still works for me I can copy it here. It is a very basic pyramid plot structure for a nine-chapter, circa 6,000–10,000 word story working on a very basic plot:

- The opening
- The arrival of conflict
- The early achievement
- The twist and change
- The denouement
- The final outcome.

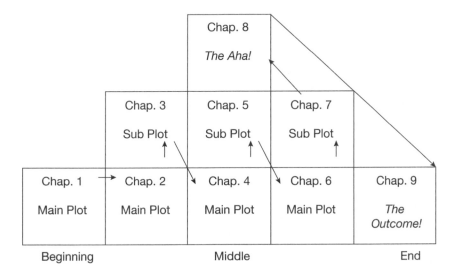

Try to follow the numbers. The 'aha' may look a little out of place perched on top there but that is because it is the king of the castle, it is the big issue, everything else has been setting it up, hence its positioning. Looking at this in a linear fashion, it would look like this:

Beginning

Chapter 1	Main plot	Introduce the main *hook*, characters and problem
Chapter 2	Main plot	Develop the characters, hook, plot and dilemma
Chapter 3	Sub plot	Introduce distraction, partial/early achievement

Introduce the Inciting Incident

Middle

Cause and effect/action and reaction

| Chapter 4 | Main plot | Return to problem and develop it getting worse |

Chapter 5	Sub plot	Engage with the main plot in the problem development
Chapter 6	Main plot	The problem/crisis is reaching its peak
Chapter 7	Sub/main plot	Intertwine as the crisis peaks

Introduce the Closing Incident

End

| Chapter 8 | The aha! | The problem/crisis is concluded/solved |

Draw to a close

| Chapter 9 | The outcome! | The end of the book |

As you can see, this system could be reduced for a smaller book and increased for a larger book, contending with a longer main plot and more than one sub-plot. And knowing roughly what each box will contain by writing a short thumbnail sketch or outline allows you to plan the story in advance.

But remember, there are a number of issues you need to consider when mapping your plot out. For example:

- Keep the story moving forward, keep thinking about 'what happens next' and don't get bogged down in over extending the prose. What matters is the story not your verbal dexterity – although that does not mean you cannot use language well.
- Are the next pages worth turning? After a bright start, if your story has already started to sag in the middle, are you sure you are writing the story you intend? All of us are guilty of writing into the story by taking threads which are distracting from the main thrust of the action. I always think of this as walking with one foot on the road and one in the ditch: it can be OK for a while but at some point you need to get back on the road. And if you find yourself in the ditch, well, that is where the story will remain.
- Are you showing or telling the story? The show–not–tell problem is ever in evidence.

Chapter 19

The oil on the water

I began this book by saying that if you mention the idea of writing for 'early years' in most social or academic circles the immediate reaction is usually that you are writing about little books for little people. But the complexities surrounding such a discourse are much thornier than this simple explanation provides. The cult and culture that surrounds and tries to define a child and childhood is a highly developed industry and a lot of the critical material targeted at the practice of adult-produced culture for children (in books, film, stage and television) overlaps with this wider picture on critical and cultural transmission and the complexities of the cultural field of production, which cannot be separated or critiqued in isolation from many of the other component parts. But I am with Maurice Sendak when he says that he perceives children to be 'intuitively aware' of what goes on around them.[1] And if we too maintain a critically creative and creatively critical vigilance and become more aware, then child-centred culture can be a force for good. I firmly believe that and I hope you will agree I have addressed this at length. Of course the ideas I have proposed will have critics and critical responses. But that is to be hoped because closure breeds tyranny and I am leaving the door ajar. Explore at will, if you will.

But what I hope I have also done is help make some connections which show that children are more able to make the connections for themselves. Story, especially fiction, is a site for and of exploration and is immensely significant in terms of building a sense of identity, capacity and sense of self. But, and sometimes I feel like shouting this from tall towers, as artists and writers engaged in child-centred culture, communication and media we need to be aware, because the terms of what we write should be negotiated around such information. And I repeat (I am doing a lot of repeating in this book but needs must) the writer and the reader; the artist and the audience are involved in a shared project. In this shared project too, the adult, the writer, the artist must ask himself or herself not *am I a good storyteller?* but *what kind of person do I want to be?* Because when you are faced with your reader, there will be many (especially critics) who will queue up to offer an answer to the first. Faced with the second question, however, as Phillips reveals, 'there may be terrors but there are no experts' (1995). But in light of the research revealed above, it also asks: what kind of person do you want your reader to be and to become?

It isn't enough to say you have no choice in this matter, child-centred art and culture is not about commodity or indulgence. Like all art it is about saying something new; and in this case something that a child has yet to experience. A child comes to a book or a picture or a play (say) for reaffirmation of what they already know but also to experience that which they know not. As Josi Arnold reveals, 'Umberto Eco has a very interesting take on this. That is, that "the universe of literature" serves a moral function through allowing an externalised yet intimate and personal examination of truth' (Arnold 2010). Eco follows this statement with,

> the wretches who roam around aimlessly and kill people by throwing stones from a highway bridge or setting fire to a child . . . turn out this way . . . because they are excluded from the universe of literature and from those places where, through education and discussion, they might be reached by a glimmer from the world of values that stems from and sends us back again to books.
>
> (Eco 2006: 4)

This is hugely optimistic, but why shouldn't it be? As I have also written elsewhere, it shouldn't matter what television, the internet, 24/7 media etc. throw at children: if we can keep them in the story loop which is so huge in their education, so we can teach them to think about the stories that will make up the connections in their lives; stories that define their existence; the rich intertextuality of their lives; the narrative that sustains their continuing sense of being in the communities in which we all of us co-exist, so that they may question the issues that threaten them – poverty, inequality, poor ethics, maltreatment and so on. If we give up challenging the story, intervening in the narrative, we allow the dictators, tyrants and despots the last word – the world's children deserve better. That is what adult-produced, child-centred discourse should be all about! I have tried to relate this by taking you through a small tour of some connecting, critical fragments – it has been a bit random but in doing so I hope I have made a connection (Melrose 2010).

I understand there are some out there who might say the optimistic stance taken in this book is merely a very small, rainbow-coloured, oil slick floating on the surface of a big sea, but what is the alternative? Giving up and leaving the children scrabbling around in the dark[2] doesn't seem a credible alternative, surely?

I cannot say that is the answer. This is not the age of post-childhood. As Bhabha explained as the new millennium approached:

> If the jargon of our times – postmodernity, postcoloniality, postfeminism – has any meaning at all, it does not lie in the popular use of the 'post' to indicate sequentiality – *after*-feminism; or polarity – *anti*-modernism. These terms that insistently gesture to the beyond, only embody its restless and revisionary energy if they transform the present into an expanded and ex-centric site of experience and empowerment.
>
> (Bhabha 1994: 4)

Of course, it is all very well discussing such things as 'revisionary energy' and a 'site of experience and empowerment' in theoretical speak, as I have done, although I did try and expand in the *Kyoto* story. But as I said at the start, Deleuze is right here to say,

> The relationships between theory and practice are far more partial and fragmentary. Practice is a set of relays from one theoretical point to another, and theory is a relay from one practice to another. No theory can develop without eventually encountering a wall, and practice is necessary for piercing this wall.
>
> (Deleuze, in Foucault and Deleuze 1972: 2)

So let me say one final thing: every story for children should end with the promise of a new beginning. I end so you can begin, for, as wise Harold Rosen once wrote, 'Sentences end with full stops. Stories do not!' (Rosen 1985).

The end, which is just the beginning . . .

Notes

Introduction

1 Those who are interested in the intricacies of these ideas should read Sonia Livingstone's *Children and the Internet*, Cambridge, Polity Press, 2009.

1 Monsters under the bed

1 See Maria Nikolajeva, *Power, Voice and Subjectivity in Literature for Young Readers* (2010: 1).
2 I find this chapter by Kimberley Reynolds extremely useful on this issue.
3 I appreciate and acknowledge the helpful conversation I had with Prof. Jen Webb, University of Canberra, on this issue.
4 TEXT vol 14, no 1, April 2010.

2 Picture books (re)defined

1 Foucault, Michel 2001 *Fearless Speech* (trans. Joseph Pearson), Cambridge, MA: Semiotext(e).
2 Picture by Stephanie Morris © 2011, reproduced by permission.
3 Penelope in *The Odyssey* is Odysseus's wife awaiting his return from the Trojan war. In order to remain faithful to her husband she fends off her suitors by saying she will not choose one of them until she has finished weaving a burial shroud for Odysseus's elderly father Laertes. It's a little trick, because every night she undoes part of the shroud and starts again the next morning.

3 Life in the distillery

1 There is nothing magical about the number 32 in the picture book process. It has all to do with economy and the way paper is produced and cut – 32 pages makes maximum use and minimum waste of paper.
2 'Bertold Brecht against György Lukács', *Aesthetics and Politics Debates Between Bloch, Lukács, Brecht, Benjamin and Adorno*, trans. Ronald Taylor, London: Verso, 1977.

5 The language of words, images and (in)completeness

1 We both love the original but agree the best laughs are in the Muppets version, *The Muppet Christmas Carol*, 1992, Dir. Brian Henson.
2 It is only an anecdotal point but I once heard it expressed that Google contained more white noise than useful information and I rather like the analogy.
3 See Reynolds 2007.
4 © A Melrose 2010 – and the answer is no, I didn't eat it but I did have some fantastic Japanese noodles on that trip.
5 http://www.mydaily.co.uk/2011/03/31/hello-boys-wonderbra-billboard-voted-most-iconic-advert-image-of-all-time/

6 © Andrew Melrose 2010.
7 © Andrew Melrose 2010.
8 http://www.8notes.com/school/riffs/images/beethoven_symphony5.gif
9 © Andrew Melrose 2010.
10 © Chaco Kato 2011 and reproduced with permission.
11 Read more: http://www.theage.com.au/entertainment/art-and-design/trash-art-that-is-not-here-to-stay-20110524-1f2cp.html#ixzz1NdfRqrlN
12 © Jen Webb 2011, previously unpublished poems, and reproduced with permission.
13 © Jen Webb 2011 and reproduced with permission.
14 http://www.brightonpride.org/
15 See Banksey's book (2005) *Wall and Piece*, London, Century, for examples of his work.
16 It is a real place in West Sussex, UK http://www.fulkingvillage.co.uk/
17 © This is a personal snap of a junction on a road in Devon, UK – the home of Inner and Outer Hope which was sent to me but which I have been unable to source, even although every effort has been made to do so. FYI, I chose the Hope and Anchor.

6 Counterpointing corrections

1 Herodotus estimates that Homer lived 400 years before Herodotus' own time, which would place *The Iliad* and *The Odyssey* at around 850 BC but this date is contested; some say the twelfth century BC and its interesting just trying to trace what information we have on this.
2 Call me sentimental but Harold Rosen is Michael Rosen's father, so mentioning them both in the same book surely deserves recognition.
3 © Andrew Melrose 2011.
4 Natascha Biebow now runs *Blue Elephant Storyshaping* http://www.blueelephantstoryshaping.com/ and she has a huge amount of experience in picture book production.
5 © Andrew Melrose 2010.
6 Pieter Bruegel de Oude, *Landscape with the Fall of Icarus* (c. 1558). Image accessed Wikimedia Commons 2010 http://commons.wikimedia.org/wiki/File:Bruegel,_Pieter_de_Oude_-_De_val_van_icarus_-_hi_res.jpg).
7 Jacques Derrida, *Writing and Difference*, trans. Alan Bass, Routledge, 1978, p. 279.
8 © Andrew Melrose 2010.

7 More mosters and bears

1 You can see Michael Rosen performing it here, http://www.youtube.com/watch?v=ytc0U2WAz4s
2 See Booker.
3 Coleridge coined the phrase in his *Biographia Literaria*, published in 1817 when talking about the *Lyrical Ballads*. The notion of such an action by an audience was, however, recognised well before this, especially with the concerns of Horace in his *Ars Poetica*.
4 I have tried to source the original quotation link to a website at the University of Birmingham, UK, without success.
5 Freud 1915.
6 I know Jack Zipes talks about American culture in this context but I have seen enough of the USA, Europe and Australasia to suggest this is way bigger than confining it to the USA suggests.

8 Know the reading child

1 http://www.notoagebanding.org/ accessed May 2011.
2 Op. cit.
3 http://www.notoagebanding.org/index.php?pullman accessed May 2011.
4 http://www.philip-pullman.com/about.asp accessed January 2011.
5 http://www.randomhouse.co.uk/catalog/bookcb.htm?command=Search&db=main.txt&eqisbndata=0099434180 accessed May 2011.

9 Crossing the border

1 I have yet to source this but Enid Blyton is said to have insisted that children did not like the first person narrative voice and therefore chose not to use it.
2 R. Burch (2005) 'Phenomenology, Lived Experience: Taking a Measure of the Topic', *Phenomenology & Pedagogy*, 8: 130-60, www.phenomenologyonline.com/articles/burch2.html accessed March 2011.
3 Foucault, Michel (2001) *Fearless Speech* (trans. Joseph Pearson), Cambridge MA: Semiotext(e).
4 *Thoughts for the Times on War and Death*, Sigmund Freud 1915.

10 Considering the monsters

1 Man 1986: 91.
2 I found Homi Bhabha's work on Walter Benjamin's ideas on translation, especially the essay 'How Newness Enters the World', in *The Location of Culture*, pp. 212–35, extremely useful here.
3 Chris Powling, in *Twentieth Century Writers*, edition Tracy Chevalier, St James Press, 1978, third ed. 1989.
4 http://www.burningtheclocks.co.uk/ accessed May 2011, picture reproduced by permission © John Varah, artistic director, Same Sky.
5 See Fredrich Jameson, "Postmodernism and Consumer Society", in *Postmodern Culture*, ed. Hal Foster, Pluto Press, 1985, p. 119.
6 For a fuller explanation on this idea see Webb 2010, http://aawp.org.au/files/Icarus%202%20Webb.pdf

11 Surprise

1 With apologies to Otis Redding, but it is a musical story.
2 'Dialectics at a standstill – this is the quintessence of the method': Walter Benjamin, *The Arcades Project*, ed. Rolf Tiedemann, trans. Howard Eiland and Kevin McLaughlin, Cambridge: Belknap/Harvard UP, 1999: 865.
3 This poem was written especially for my Professorial Inaugural Address, where I was dealing with different ways of conveying a story. I had been recalling the time in my youth when I hitched a lift on a boat sailing to Iona, on the west coast of Scotland, and a whale surfaced alongside us. It seemed right to use the language of my birth, for the full address see, 'Jesus, Judas, Jimi and John: culture, communication, media and art in delightful chaos', TEXT, 14(1).

13 Story structure and characters

1 http://www.randomhouse.com/features/pullman/author/carnegie.html

14 Picture books illustrated

1 The two illustrations by Karenanne Knight, 2010, reproduced by permission.
2 *Kyoto* was written by Andrew Melrose and illustrated by Karenanne Knight. It began as an exercise between a PhD student (KK) and her tutor (AM) – see, '*Kyoto*: A Collaborative Project between a Student (GRA) and her Supervisor (AM)' in *New Writing: The International Journal for the Practice and Theory of Creative Writing*, 5(1) (2007): 41–9.

15 Voice and point of view (POV)

1 http://learnenglishkids.britishcouncil.org/en/short-stories/little-red-riding-hood
2 A gag paraphrased from Peter Schaefer's *Amadeus* with apologies.

16 Dialogue, rhythm and rhyme

1 I cannot rehearse the idea of child, language and literacy here for it would take a whole book to do so but there are others who have already approached this.

2 M. M. Bakhtin, 'Discourses in the Novel', *The Dialogic Imagination Four Essays*, ed. M. Holquist, trans. C. Emerson, Austin: University of Texas Press, 1981 – for an explanation see Rudd 2010: 165.

3 It is somewhat serendipitous but as I wrote this Julia Donaldson was made the Children's Laureate in the UK.

17 Story

1 © Stephanie Morris, 2011, reproduced with permission.

19 The oil on the water

1 See Zomeds 2001: 171–92.

2 © Jen Webb 2011 and reproduced with permission.

Some useful websites

http://www.wordpool.co.uk/wfc/wfc.htm
http://www.booktrustchildrensbooks.org.uk/Features-Interviews
www.write4children.org
www.cwteaching.com
http://britishscbwi.jimdo.com/
http://www.irscl.com/

www.cool-reads.co.uk
www.achuka.co.uk
www.literacytrust.org.uk

Bibliography

Abbs, Peter (1996) *The Polemics of Imagination*, London: Skoob Books.

Adorno, Theodor (1991) *The Culture Industry*, London: Routledge.

Althusser, Louis (1966) 'Letter to D' (18 July 1966), in Olivier Corpet and François Matheron (eds), *Writings on Psychoanalysis: Freud and Lacan*, trans. Jeffrey Mehlman, New York: Columbia University Press.

Althusser, L. and Balibar, E. (1997) *Reading Capital*, trans. B. Brewster, London: Verso.

Appleyard, J. A. (1994) *Becoming a Reader: The Experience of Fiction from Childhood to Adulthood*, Cambridge: Cambridge University Press.

Arendt, Hannah (1999 [1958]), *The Human Condition*, revised 1999, Chicago, IL: Chicago University Press.

Armstrong, Karen (2005) *A Short History of Myth*, Edinburgh: Canongate Books.

Arnold, Josie (2010) 'The Liminal and Apophatic Voice of the Writer in/as Autobiography: A Subjective Academic Narrative', *TEXT*, 14(1).

Auden, W. H. (1963) *The Dyer's Hand, and Other Essays*, London: Faber & Faber.

Auerbach, Erich (1998) *Mimesis: The Representation of Reality in Western Literature*, trans. Willard Trask, Cambridge, MA: Harvard University Press.

Bader, Barbara (1976) *American Picturebooks from Noah's Ark to the Beast Within*, New York: Macmillan.

Bakhtin, Mikhail (1984) *Rabelais and his World*, trans. H. Iswolsky, Bloomington: Indiana University Press.

Bakhtin, Mikhail (1990) *Art and Answerability: Early Philosophical Essays*, ed. by M. Holquist and V. Liapunov, trans. V. Liapunov, Austin: University of Texas Press.

Bakhtin, Mikhail (2008 [1981]) 'Discourses in the Novel', in M. Holquist (ed.) *The Dialogic Imagination Four Essays*, trans. C. Emerson and M. Holquist, Austin: University of Texas Press.

Bakhtin, Mikhail (2010 [1986]) *Speech Genres and Other Late Essays*, ed. by C. Emerson and M. Holquist, trans. V. McGee, Austin: University of Texas Press.

Bal, M. (1997) *Narratology: Introduction to the Theory of Narrative*, second edition, Toronto and London: University of Toronto Press.

Barthes, Roland (1975) *The Pleasure of the Text*, trans. Richard Miller, London: Hill and Wang.

Barthes, Roland (1977) 'Death of the Author,' *Image, Music, Text*, trans. R. Howard, http://evans-experientialism.freewebspace.com/barthes06.htm (accessed February 2011).

Batchelor, S. A., Kitzinger, J. and Burtney, E. (2004) 'Representing Young People's Sexuality in the "Youth" Media', *Health Education Research*, 19(6).

Baudrillard, Jean (1993) *The Transparency of Evil: Essays on Extreme Phenomena*, trans. J. Benedict, London: Verso.

Bearne, Eve (1966) *Differentiation and Diversity in the Primary School*, London: Routledge.

Belsey, Catherine (2005) *Culture and the Real: Theorizing Cultural Criticism*, London: Routledge.

Benjamin, Walter (1973) *Illuminations*, trans. Harry Zohn, ed. with an Introduction by Hannah Arendt, London: Fontana.

Benjamin, Walter (1999) *The Arcades Project*, ed. Rolf Tiedemann, trans. Howard Eiland and Kevin McLaughlin, Cambridge: Belknap/Harvard University Press.

Benjamin, Walter (2006 [1979]) *One-Way Street*, trans. J. A. Underwood, London and New York: Verso Classics.

Bennett, T. (1983) 'Text Readers, Reading Formation,' *The Bulletin of the Midwest Modern Language Association,* 16(1) (Spring): 13–17 (accessed via Jstor www.jstor.org/stable/1314830 January 2011).

Bettelheim, Bruno (1976) *The Uses of Enchantment: The Meaning and Importance of Fairy Tales,* New York: Knopf.

Bhabha, Homi K. (ed.) (1990) *Nation and Narration*. London and New York: Routledge.

Bhabha, Homi K. (2004 [1994]) *The Location of Culture,* London: Routledge Classics.

Blake, Andrew (2000) 'Of More Than Academic Interest: C. S. Lewis and the Golden Age', in M. Carretero-Gonzalez and E. Hidalgo Tenorio (eds) *Behind the Veil of Familiarity: C. S. Lewis (1898–1998)*, Bern and Oxford: Peter Lang.

Blanchot, M. (1999) *Blanchot Reader: Fiction and Literary Essays*, ed. by G. Quasla, trans. L. Davis, P. Auster and R. Lamberton, New York: Station Hill.

Booker, Christopher (2004) *The Seven Basic Plots: Why We Tell Stories*, London: Continuum.

Booth, Wayne (1983) *The Rhetoric of Fiction*, Chicago, IL: University of Chicago Press (Penguin reprint 1991).

Boulter, Amanda (2007) *Writing Fiction Creative and Critical Approaches*, Basingstoke: Palgrave Macmillan.

Bourdieu, Pierre (2000) *Pascalian Meditations*, trans. R. Nice, Cambridge: Polity Press.

Bourdieu, Pierre (2004 [1993]) *The Field of Popular Culture,* ed. by R. Johnson, Cambridge: Polity Press.

Brande, D. (1996 [1934]) *Becoming a Writer*, London: Palgrave Macmillan.

Brecht, Bertold (1977) 'Bertold Brecht Against György Lukács', *Aesthetics and Politics Debates between Bloch, Lukács, Brecht, Benjamin and Adorno*, trans. Ronald Taylor, London: Verso.

Butler, R. J. and Green, D. (2007) *The Child Within: Taking the Young Person's Perspective by Applying Personal Construct Psychology*, second edition, Chichester: Wiley.

Butt, M. (ed.) (2007) *Story: The Heart of the Matter*, London: Greenwich Exchange.

Calvino, Italo (1974) *Invisible Cities*, trans. William Weaver, New York: Harcourt Brace.

Calvino, Italo (1982) *The Uses of Literature,* trans. P. Creagh, San Diego and New York: Harvest Books.

Calvino, Italo (1996 [1988]) *Six Memos for the Next Millennium,* trans. P. Creagh, London and New York: Vintage.

Carpenter, Humphrey (1985) *Secret Gardens: The Golden Age of Children's Literature*, London: Allen and Unwin.

Carter, James (ed.) (1999) *Talking Books*, London: Routledge.

Carter, R. A. (1997) *Investigating English Discourse: Language, Literacy and Literature*, London: Routledge.

Chambers, Aiden (1985) *Booktalk: Occasional Writing on Literature and Children*, London: Bodley Head.

Chambers, Aiden (1993) *Tell Me: Children, Reading and Talk*, Stroud: Thimble Press.

Chambers, Nancy (ed.) (1980) *'Signal' Approach to Children's Books*, Stroud: Thimble Press.

Chevalier, Tracy (1989) *Twentieth Century Children's Writers*, third edition, Chicago, IL: St James Press.

Chomsky, Noam (1971) *Problems of Knowledge and Freedom*, New York: Vintage.

Cianciolo, P. (1970) *Illustrations in Children's Books*, Dubuque, Iowa: Wm. C. Brown.

Colebrook, Claire (2002) *Gilles Deleuze*, London: Routledge.

Cowan, Andrew (2011) 'Blind Spots: What Creative Writing Doesn't Know', *TEXT*, 15(1), http://www.textjournal.com.au/april11/cowan.htm

Crook, C. *Theories of Formal and Informal Learning in the World of Web2.0.*, http://www.education.ox.ac.uk/esrcseries/uploaded/08_0314%20ESRC%20report_web.pdf

Danahaer, G., Schirato, T. and Webb, J. (2000) *Understanding Foucault,* London: Sage.

De Bono, Edward (1972) *Children Solve Problems,* London: Allen Lane.

De Certeau, M. (2010 [1986]) *Heterologies: Discourse on the Other,* trans. B. Massumi, Minneapolis and London: Minnesota Press.

De Man, Paul (1986) *The Resistance to Theory,* Manchester: Manchester University Press.

Deleuze, Gilles (1994) *Difference and Repetition,* trans. Paul Patton, London: Athlone.

Deleuze, G. and Guattari, F. (2004 [1980]) *A Thousand Plateaus,* London: Continuum.

Derrida, Jacques (1978) *Writing and Difference,* trans. Alan Bass, London: Routledge.

Derrida, Jacques (1982) *Margins of Philosophy,* Chicago, IL: University of Chicago Press.

Derrida, Jacques (2002) 'The Law of Genre', in Derek Attridge (ed.), *Acts of Literature,* New York: Routledge, pp. 221–52.

Donaldson, Julia and Scheffler, Axel (1999) *The Gruffalo,* London: Macmillan.

Eaton, Anthony (2010) 'Growing Older: Young Adult Fiction Coming of Age,' *Writing in Education,* 52, (November).

Eco, Umberto (2006 [2002]) *On Literature,* trans. M. McLaughline, London: Vintage.

Eliot, T. S. (1944) *Four Quartets,* London: Faber & Faber.

Fanon, Franz (1986) *Black Skin, White Masks,* London: Pluto.

Farjeon, Eleanor (1935) 'Writing "for" Children', *The Writer's Desk Book,* London: A&C Black.

Fearne, M. (ed.) (1985) *'Only The Best Is Good Enough',* The Woodfield Lectures on Children's Literature 1978–1985, London: Rossendale.

Fiske, John (1989) *Understanding Popular Culture,* London: Unwin Hyman.

Foucault, Michel (1970) *The Order of Things,* trans. Alan Sheridan, New York: Pantheon.

Foucault, Michel (1979 [1977]) 'The Life of Infamous Men', in Meaghan Morris and Paul Patton (eds), *Michel Foucault: Power, Truth, Strategy,* trans. Paul Foss and Meaghan Morris, Sydney: Feral Publications.

Foucault, Michel (1991) *Discipline and Punish: The Birth of the Prison,* trans. A. Sheridan, London: Penguin.

Foucault, Michel (1998 [1976]) *The Will to Knowledge: The History of Sexuality: 1,* London and New York: Penguin.

Foucault, Michel (2002 [1994]) *Power: Essential Works of Foucault 1954–84, Volume 3,* ed. by J. Faubion, London: Penguin.

Foucault, Michel (2008) *The Birth of Biopolitics: Lectures at the Collège de France 1978–1979,* ed. by M. Senellart, F. Ewald, A. Fontana and A. I. Davidson, trans. G. Burchell, Basingstoke and New York: Palgrave Macmillan.

Foucault, Michel and Deleuze, Gilles (1972) 'Intellectuals and Power: A Conversation between Michel Foucault and Gilles Deleuze', http://www.libcom.org/library/intellectuals-power-a-conversation-between-michel-foucault-and-gilles-deleuze (accessed April 2010).

Freud, Sigmund (1915) 'Thoughts for the Times on War and Death', in *The Standard Edition of the Complete Psychological Works of Sigmund Freud* (1953–74), trans. James Strachey, in collaboration with Anna Freud, assisted by Alix Strachey and Alan Tyson, London: Hogarth Press, pp. 273–300.

Freud, Sigmund (1983) 'Three Essays on Sexuality', in *On Sexuality, Volume 7*: Penguin Freud Library, Harmondsworth: Penguin.

Freud, Sigmund (1990) *Art and Literature,* London: Penguin.

Freud, Sigmund (1995) *The Freud Reader,* ed. P. Gray, London: Vintage Originals.

Frey, James (1987) *How to Write a Damn Good Novel,* London: St Martins Press.

Friel, J. (2000) 'Reading as a Writer', in J. Newman, J. E. Cusick and A. La Tourette (eds) (2000) *The Writer's Workbook,* London: Hodder Arnold.

Fukuyama, Francis (1992) *The End of History and the Last Man*, New York: The Free Press.

Gardener, J. (1991) *The Art of Fiction*, New York: Vintage Books.

Gilligan, Carol (1982) *In a Different Voice*, Cambridge, MA: Harvard University Press.

Goldthwaite, J. (1996) *The Natural History of Make Believe: A Guide to the Principal Works of Britain, Europe and America,* New York and Oxford: Oxford University Press.

Gordon, J. (1975) *The Thorny Paradise: Writer's on Writing for Children,* ed. by E. Blishen, Harmondsworth: Kestrel.

Goswami, U. (2008) *Byron Review on the Impact of New Technologies on Children: A Research Literature Review: Child Development*, Cambridge: Cambridge University Press.

Grenby, M. O. (2008) *Children's Literature*, Edinburgh: Edinburgh University Press.

Grenby, M. O. and Immel, A. (eds) (2009) *The Cambridge Companion to Children's Literature*, Cambridge: Cambridge University Press.

Griffiths, M. (1995) *Feminisms and the Self: The Web of Identity,* London: Routledge.

Hall, Stuart (ed.) (1980) *Culture, Media, Language*, London: Hutchinson.

Hardy, G. H. (1940) *A Mathematician's Apology*, Cambridge: Cambridge University Press.

Hazard, P. (1947) *Books, Children and Men*, Boston: The Horn Book.

Heaney, S. (1979) *Preoccupations: Selected Prose 1968–78*, London: Faber & Faber.

Hollindale, Peter (1988) *Ideology and the Children's Book,* Stroud: Thimble Press.

Hollindale, Peter (1997) *Signs of Childness in Children's Books*, Stroud: Thimble Press.

hooks, bel (2000) 'Remembered Rapture: Dancing with Words', *Journal of Advanced Composition*, 20(1) (Winter): 1–8.

Hourihan, Marjorie (1997) *Deconstructing the Hero*, London: Routledge.

Hughes, T. (1968) *Poetry in the Making*, London: Faber & Faber.

Hull, R. (2001) 'What Hope for Children's Poetry?', *Books for Keeps*, January.

Hunt, Peter (1994) *An Introduction to Children's Literature*, Oxford: Oxford University Press.

Hunt, Peter (2001) *Children's Literature*, Oxford: Blackwell.

Hunt, Peter (ed.) (2004) *International Companion Encyclopaedia of Children's Literature*, London: Routledge Farmer.

Hunt, Peter (ed.) (2010 [2005]) *Understanding Children's Literature,* second edition, London: Routledge.

Inglis, Fred (1981) *The Promise of Happiness, Value and Meaning in Children's Fiction*, Cambridge: Cambridge University Press.

Irigaray, Luce (1985) *This Sex Which Is Not One,* trans. C. Porter, Ithaca, NY: Cornell University Press.

Irigaray, Luce (2008) *Sharing the World,* London: Continuum.

Irigaray, Luce (2008) *Teaching*, ed. by M. Green, London: Continuum.

James, A. and Prout, A. (eds) (2000 [1997]) *Constructing and Deconstructing Childhood: Contemporary Issues in the Sociological Study of Childhood,* London: Routledge.

James, A., Jenks, C. and Prout, A. (1998) *Theorizing Childhood*, Cambridge: Polity Press.

James, K. (2009) *Death, Gender And Sexuality in Contemporary Adolescent Literature*, London: Routledge.

Jameson, Fredric (1981) *The Political Unconscious: Narrative as a Socially Symbolic Act*, Ithaca, NY: Cornell University Press.

Jameson, Fredric (1991) *Postmodernism or the Cultural Logic of Late Capitalism*, London: Verso.

Jenkins, H. (ed.) (1998) *The Children's Culture Reader*, New York: New York University Press.

Kant, I. (1997 [1790]) *Critique of Judgment*, trans. W. S. Pluhar, Indianapolis: Hackett.

Krauth, Nigel (2006) 'The Domains of the Writing Process,' in T. Brady and N. Krauth, *Creative Writing: Theory beyond Practice,* Teneriffe, Qld.: Post Pressed.

Kristeva, J. (1998) 'Revolution in poetic language', in Paul du Gay, Jessica Evans and Peter Redman (eds), *Identity: A Reader* (2000), London: Sage.

Kundera, Milan (2000 [1968]) *The Art of the Novel,* trans. L. Asher, London: Faber & Faber.

Kundera, Milan (2007) *The Curtain: An Essay in Seven Parts,* trans. L. Asher, London: Faber & Faber.

Lacan, Jacques (1953) 'Some Reflections on the Ego', *International Journal of Psychoanalysis*, 34.

Leeson, Robert (1985) *Reading and Righting,* London: Collins.

Lesnik-Oberstein, Karen (ed.) (2004) *Children's Literature: New Approaches*, Basingstoke: Palgrave Macmillan.

Livingstone, Sonia (2009) *Children and the Internet*, Cambridge: Polity Press.

Lowe, Virginia (2007) *Stories, Pictures and Reality: Two Children Tell,* London and New York: Routledge.

Malouf, D. (1996) Interviewed by Jan Dalley in the *Independent on Sunday* (4 August), http://www.independent.co.uk/arts-entertainment/books/books-king-of-the-wild-1308181.html (accessed 15 November 2010).

McCaw, N. (2011) 'Close Reading, Writing and Culture', *New Writing: The International Journal for the Practice and Theory of Creative Writing,* 8(1): 25–34.

McCloud, Scott (1993) *Understanding Comics*, Northampton, MA: Undra.

McGillis, R. (1997) 'Learning to Read, Reading to Learn; or Engaging in Critical Pedagogy', *Children's Literature Association Quarterly*, 22(3) (Fall): 126–32.

McKee, Robert (1999) *Story*, London: Methuen.

Meek, Margaret (1988) *How Texts Teach What Readers Learn*, Stroud: Thimble Press.

Meek, Margaret, Warlow, Aiden and Barton, Griselda (1977) *The Cool Web*, London: Bodley Head.

Melrose, Andrew (2001) *Storykeeping: The Story, the Child and the Word*, Carlisle: Paternoster.

Melrose, Andrew (2002) *Write For Children*, London and New York: Routledge.

Melrose, Andrew (2007) 'Reading and Righting: Carrying on the "Creative Writing Theory" Debate', *New Writing: The International Journal for the Practice and Theory of Creative Writing*, 4(2).

Melrose, Andrew (2010) *Jesus, Judas, Jimi and John: Culture, Communication, Media and Art in Delightful Chaos, TEXT*, 14(1).

Melrose, Andrew (2011a) *Here Comes the Bogeyman: Exploring Contemporary Issues in Writing for Children*, London: Routledge.

Melrose, Andrew (2011b) 'Icarus in ellipses . . . some thoughts on textual intervention', http://aawp.org.au/files/Icarus%201%20Melrose.pdf (accessed April 2011).

Melrose, Andrew and Harbour, Vanessa (2007) 'Junk, Skunk and Northern Lights: Representation of Drugs in Children's Literature', in Paul Manning (ed.), *Drugs and Popular Culture: Drugs, Media and Identity in Contemporary Society,* Cullompton: Willan Publishing.

Melrose, Andrew and Webb, Jen (2011) 'Intimacy and the Icarus Effect', publication pending in *Axon: Creative Explorations* (ISSN 1838–8973).

Melrose, A., Webb, J., Kroll, J. and May, S. (2010) *Icarus Extended*, Brighton: Lulu.

Nabokov, V. (2010 [1936]) *Laughter in the Dark*, London: Penguin Modern Classics.

Natov, Roni (2006) *The Poetics of Childhood*, London: Routledge.

Nietzsche, Friedrich (1993 [1872]) *The Birth of Tragedy out of the Spirit of Music*, trans. Shaun Whiteside, London: Penguin.

Nikolajeva, Maria (2005) *Aesthetic Approaches to Children's Literature: An Introduction,* Oxford: The Scarecrow Press.

Nikolajeva, Maria (2010) *Power, Voice and Subjectivity in Literature for Young Readers*, London and New York: Routledge.

Nodelman, Perry (1988) *Words about Pictures: The Narrative Art of Children's Books*, Athens: University of Georgia Press.

Nodelman, Perry (2008) *The Hidden Adult: Defining Children's Literature,* Baltimore, MD: Johns Hopkins University Press.

Orwell, George (2000) *Essays*, London and New York: Penguin.

Phillips, Adam (1995) *Terrors and Experts,* London: Faber & Faber.

Phillips, Adam (2000) *Promises, Promises*, London: Faber & Faber.

Phillips, Adam (2002) *Equals*, London: Faber & Faber.

Powling, Chris (ed.) (1994) *The Best of Books for Keeps*, London: Bodley Head.

Pullman, Philip (1996) 'Carnegie Medal Acceptance Speech', www.randomhouse.com/features/pullman/author/carnegie (accessed 19 July 2011).

Pullman, Philip (2011) http://www.sfcrowsnest.com/articles/features/2008/The-Shadow-In-The-North-12032.php (accessed 20 June 2011).

Reynolds, Kimberley (2007) *Radical Children's Literature: Future Visions and Aesthetic Transformations in Juvenile Fiction,* Basingstoke and New York: Palgrave Macmillan.

Reynolds, Kimberley (2009) 'Transformative Energies', in Janet Maybin and Nicola Watson (eds), *Children's Literature Approaches and Territories,* Basingstoke: Palgrave Macmillan.

Richards, I. A. (1954) *How to Read a Page: A Course in Effective Reading with an Introduction to a Hundred Great Words*, London: Routledge & Kegan Paul.

Richardson, L. (1991) *Writing Strategies: Reaching Diverse Audiences*, London: Sage.

Ricour, Paul (1965) *History and Truth*, trans. Chas. A. Kelbley, Chicago, IL: Northwestern University Press.

Rorty, Richard (1989) *Contingency, Irony and Solidarity*, Cambridge: Cambridge University Press.

Rorty, Richard (1998) *Achieving Our Country*, Cambridge, MA: Harvard University Press.

Rose, Jacqueline (1984) *The Case of Peter Pan or The Impossibility of Children's Fiction*, revised edition, London: Macmillan.

Rosen, Harold (1985) *Stories and Meanings*, Stroud, Thimble Press.

Ross, Stephen (ed.) (2009) *Modernism and Theory: A Critical Debate*, London: Routledge.

Rudd, David (ed.) (2010) *The Routledge Companion to Children's Literature*, London: Routledge.

Sarland, Charles (1996) 'Revenge of the Teenage Horrors', in Morag Styles, Eve Bearne and Victor Watson (eds) *Voices Off: Texts, Contexts and Readers*, London: Cassell Education.

Saxton, Matthew (2010) *Child Language: Acquisition and Development*, London: Sage.

Shuttleworth, Sally (1984) *George Eliot and Nineteenth-Century Science: The Make-Believe of a Beginning*, London: Cambridge University Press.

Spivak, Gayatri (1988) 'Can the Subaltern Speak?', in Cary Nelson and Lawrence Grossberg (eds) *Marxism and the Interpretation of Culture,* Urbana: University of Illinois Press.

Steedman, Carolyn (1995) *Strange Dislocations: Childhood and the Idea of Human Interiority,* Cambridge, MA: Harvard University Press.

Steig, M. (1993) 'Never Going Home: Reflections on Reading, Adulthood, and the Possibility of Children's Literature', *Children's Literature Association Quarterly*, 18(1) (Spring): 36–9.

Stewig, John Warren (1995) *Looking at Picture Books*, Fort Atkinson, WI: Highsmith Press.

Styles, Morag, Bearne, Eve and Watson, Victor (eds) (1996) *Voices Off: Texts, Contexts and Readers*, London: Cassell Education.

Taylor, Ronald (ed.) (1977) *Aesthetics and Politics: Debates between Bloch, Lukács, Brecht, Benjamin and Adorno*, London: Verso.

Trevor, W. (1990) Interviewed by D. J. R. Bruckner in the *New York Times* (21 May) http://www.nytimes.com/books/98/09/06/specials/trevor-blooming.html (accessed 15 November 2010).

Tucker, Nicholas (1981) *The Child and the Book: A Psychological and Literary Exploration,* Cambridge: Cambridge University Press.

Waddell, Martin (1991) 'Writing Texts for Picture Books', *Books for Keeps: the children's book magazine online,* http://booksforkeeps.co.uk/issue/68/childrens-books/articles/other-articles/writing-texts-for-picture-books (accessed September 2011).

Waddell, Martin and Burningham, Christian (2009) *A Kitten Called Moonlight*, London: Walker Books.

Wallen, Margaret (ed.) (1990) *Every Picture Tells . . .* Sheffield: National Association for the Teaching of English.

Watson, Victor (2000) *Reading Series Fiction*, London: Routledge.

Webb, Jen (2005) 'Undoing "the Folded Lie": Media, Art and Ethics', *New Zealand Journal of Media Studies*, Special Issue: 'Asian' Media Arts Practice in/and Aotearoa New Zealand, 9(1).

Webb, Jen (2009) *Understanding Representation,* London: Sage.

Webb, Jen (2011) Personal communication.

Webb, Jen and Krauth, Nigel (2010) 'Writing and its Intersections', *TEXT*, 14(1) (April).

Webb, Jen and Melrose, Andrew (2011) 'Intimacy and the Icarus Effect', as yet unpublished article.

Webb, J., Schirato, T. and Danaher, G. (2002) *Understanding Bourdieu*, Crows Nest, NSW: Allen & Unwin.

White, Hayden (1987) *The Content of the Form*, Baltimore, MD: Johns Hopkins University Press.

Wittgenstein, Ludwig (1980) *Remarks on the Philosophy of Psychology*, Volume I, Chicago, IL: University of Chicago Press.

Zipes, Jack (1993 [1983]) *The Trials and Tribulations of Red Riding Hood,* second edition, London and New York: Routledge.

Zipes, Jack (1995) *Creative Storytelling: Building Community, Changing Lives*, London: Routledge.

Zipes, Jack (1997) *Happily Ever After: Fairy Tales, Children and the Culture Industry*, London: Routledge.

Zipes, Jack (2002 [1988]) *The Brothers Grimm: From Enchanted Forests to the Modern World*, second edition, New York and Basingstoke: Palgrave.

Zipes, Jack (2002) *Sticks and Stones: The Troublesome Success of Children's Literature from Slovenly Peter to Harry Potter*, London and New York: Routledge.

Zipes, Jack (ed.) (2006) *The Oxford Encyclopaedia of Children's Literature*, www.oxfordreference.com/views/Entry.html?entry=t204.e3482&sm (accessed August 2007).

Zipes, Jack (2006) *Why Fairy Tales Stick,* London and New York: Routledge.

Zipes, Jack (2009) *Relentless Progress: The Reconfiguration of Children's Literature, Fairy Tales, and Storytelling*, London and New York: Routledge.

Žižek, Slavoj 2002 *Welcome to the Desert of the Real*, London: Verso.

Zornardo, J. (2001) *Inventing the Child: Culture, Ideology and the Story of Childhood*, New York and London: Garland Publishing.

Index